The Heart of the Woods

TEACHER'S EDITION
LEVEL 2

ODYSSEY An HBJ Literature Program

Sam Leaton Sebesta, General Consultant

Star Light, Star Bright
Hello and Good-bye
Where the Clouds Go
The Heart of the Woods

Under the Midnight Stars
Across Wide Fields
East of the Sun

At the Edge of the World
Ride the Silver Seas
Another Earth, Another Sky

HARCOURT BRACE JOVANOVICH, PUBLISHERS
Orlando   New York   Chicago   San Diego   Atlanta   Dallas

We do not include a Teacher's Edition automatically with each shipment of a classroom set of textbooks. We prefer to send a Teacher's Edition only when requested by the teacher or administrator concerned or by one of our representatives. A Teacher's Edition can be easily mislaid when it arrives as part of a shipment delivered to a school stockroom, and, since it contains answer materials, we want to be sure it is sent *directly* to the person who will use it or to someone concerned with the use or selection of textbooks.

If your classroom assignment changes and you no longer are using or examining this Teacher's Edition, you may wish to pass it on to a teacher who will be using it.

Acknowledgments

The publisher gratefully acknowledges the contribution of Elsa Konig Heald to the preparation of the Teacher's Edition lessons.

For permission to reprint copyrighted material, grateful acknowledgment is made to the following sources:

Atheneum Publishers: "Oh, A-Hunting We Will Go" from *Oh, A-Hunting We Will Go,* by John Langstaff. Text copyright © 1974 by John Langstaff.

The Bodley Head: From "Echo and Narcissus" in *Tales the Muses Told* by Roger Lancelyn Green. Copyright © 1965 by Roger Lancelyn Green.

Shirley Crawford, Kalispel Tribe: "Grandfather" by Shirley Crawford, © 1968 by Shirley Crawford.

The Dial Press: "I never asked for no allergy" excerpted from the book *Philip Hall Likes Me. I Reckon Maybe* by Bette Greene. Copyright © 1974 by Bette Greene.

E. P. Dutton: From "Bando" (retitled) from *My Side of the Mountain* by Jean George. Copyright © 1959 by Jean George.

Farrar, Straus and Giroux, Inc.: From "The Megrimum" (retitled) from *Kneeknock Rise* by Natalie Babbitt. Copyright © 1970 by Natalie Babbitt.

Harcourt Brace Jovanovich, Inc.: From "The Big Wind of '34" abridged from *Grandpa's Farm,* © 1965 by James Flora.

Harper & Row, Publishers, Inc.: Specified excerpt from p. 27 in *The Odyssey of Homer,* translated by Richmond Lattimore. Copyright © 1965, 1967 by Richmond Lattimore. Specified excerpt from *A Tree Grows in Brooklyn* by Betty Smith. Copyright, 1943, by Betty Smith.

Macmillan Publishing Co., Inc.: "Mix a Pancake" from *Sing-Song* by Christina G. Rossetti. Macmillan Publishing Co., Inc., 1924.

David McKay Co., Inc. and Mrs. Helen Thurber: From *Plays and How to Put Them On* by Moyne Rice Smith, © 1961 by Moyne Rice Smith. Published by Henry Z. Walck, Inc. Based on the book *The Great Quillow* by James Thurber, published by Harcourt Brace Jovanovich, Inc. Copyright © 1944 by James Thurber. Copyright © 1972 by Helen W. Thurber.

Eve Merriam: Excerpt from "Thumbprint" from *It Doesn't Always Have to Rhyme* by Eve Merriam. Copyright © 1964 by Eve Merriam.

Robert Lescher Literary Agency, Inc.: Quotes by Isaac Bashevis Singer.

Russell & Volkening, Inc. as agent for the author: From "A Wagon Load of Bricks" in *Harriet Tubman: Conductor on the Underground Railroad* by Ann Petry. Copyright © 1955 by Ann Petry.

Scholastic Magazines, Inc.: From *The Crane Maiden* by Miyoko Matsutani. Text copyright © 1968 by Parents' Magazine Press. "Teeny Tiny Ghost" from *Spooky Rhymes & Riddles* by Lilian Moore. Copyright © 1972 by Lilian Moore.

Schroder Music Company: From the song "You Can't Make a Turtle Come Out," words and music by Malvina Reynolds from *There's Music in the Air.* © Copyright 1962 Schroder Music Co. (ASCAP). All rights reserved.

Frederick Warne & Company, Inc.: From "The Jumblies" by Edward Lear.

Contents

General Consultant

Sam Leaton Sebesta is on the faculty of the University of Washington in Seattle, where he teaches reading and children's literature. A former elementary grade teacher, Dr. Sebesta has written numerous books and articles in the field of reading, and has earned national recognition for his speeches and workshops on teaching literature. From 1975 to 1979 he was a regional coordinator for Classroom Choices, a joint project of the Children's Book Council and the International Reading Association. Dr. Sebesta received his doctorate from Stanford University.

Consultants

Elaine M. Aoki is an administrator and reading specialist for the Seattle, Washington, public schools and was formerly an elementary school teacher in Auburn, Washington. She received her doctorate in reading from the University of Washington.

Willard E. Bill is an assistant professor and Director of the Indian Teacher Education Program at the University of Washington.

Sylvia Engdahl is an anthologist and author of science fiction and nonfiction for young people. She has written numerous articles on children's literature and is best known for her novel *Enchantress from the Stars,* a Newbery Honor Book.

Carolyn Horovitz is a former librarian in the Santa Monica, California, public schools and the University Elementary School at UCLA. She is the editor of the *Anthology of Children's Literature* (5th ed.) and a past member of the Newbery and Caldecott awards committees.

Daphne P. Muse is a lecturer in children's literature at Mills College in Oakland, California, and a children's book reviewer for KGO-TV (ABC).

Margaret D. Simpson is a specialist in children's books and Director of the Story Theatre Program for the Albany, California, public schools.

Consulting Educators

Sonya Blackman is an assistant manager of the Books Unlimited Cooperative and an instructor in children's literature at the University of California Extension in Berkeley. She received her master's degree in early childhood education from Sonoma State University.

Myra Cohn Livingston is an author and award-winning poet. She is Poet-in-Residence and a teacher of creative writing for the Beverly Hills Unified School District and is a Senior Instructor at the UCLA Extension.

Barre Toelken is a professor of English and Director of the Ethnic Studies Program at the University of Oregon, Eugene, Oregon. Dr. Toelken is a past president of the American Folklore Society and a former editor of the *Journal of American Folklore*.

William Anderson
Department of English
California State University
at Northridge
Northridge, California

Gwen Batey
Teacher
William F. Turnbull Middle
School
San Mateo, California

Dorothy W. Blake
Coordinator of Planning for
Media Resources and
Utilization
Division of Instructional
Planning and Development
Atlanta Public Schools
Atlanta, Georgia

Carlota Cardenas de Dwyer
Department of English
The University of Texas
at Austin
Austin, Texas

John M. Chavez
Educational Consultant
The Urban Institute for Human
Services, Inc.
San Francisco, California

Joan Cheifetz
Principal
Thornhill School
Oakland Unified School District
Oakland, California

Ann Cheleen
Teacher
H. O. Sonnesyn Elementary
School
New Hope, Minnesota

Harold Fenderson
Principal
R. V. Daniels Elementary
School
Jacksonville, Florida

Barbara Friedberg
Teacher
Martin Luther King, Jr.,
Laboratory School
Evanston, Illinois

M. Jean Greenlaw
College of Education
North Texas State University
Denton, Texas

Elsa Konig Heald
Teacher
Sun Valley Elementary School
San Rafael, California

Franklin Koontz
Teacher
Bellevue School District
Bellevue, Washington

Joanne Lincoln
Librarian, Professional Library
Atlanta Public Schools
Atlanta, Georgia

Frances Mackie
Teacher
Detroit Public Schools
Detroit, Michigan

Richard McBreen
Teacher
William F. Turnbull Middle
School
San Mateo, California

Nancy Lofton Morrow
Teacher, retired
Carmel Valley, California

Evelyn Myton-Plantillas
Resource Specialist
San Jose Unified School
District
San Jose, California

E. Renee Nathan
Director of Curriculum and
Special Projects, K-12
Lodi Unified School District
Lodi, California

Ben Nelms
Department of English and
College of Education
University of Missouri
Columbia, Missouri

Elizabeth Nelms
Teacher
Hickman High School
Columbia, Missouri

Soledad P. Newman
Department of English
Miami University
Oxford, Ohio

Kay Palmer
Teacher
Shoreline School District
Shoreline, Washington

Barbara K. Rand
Teacher
Springfield Middle School
Springfield, Pennsylvania

Beverly Remer
Teacher
New York City Public Schools
District 10
New York, New York

Doris Shriber
Teacher
William F. Turnbull Middle
School
San Mateo, California

Barbara M. Shulgold
Teacher
Vallemar Structured School
Pacifica, California

Clarice Stafford
Assistant Superintendent for
Curriculum
Wayne-Westland Schools
Wayne, Michigan

Barbara Tapolow
Teacher
P.S. 124
New York, New York

Ann Terry
School of Professional
Education
University of Houston at Clear
Lake City
Houston, Texas

Kelley Tucker
Teacher
Sun Valley Elementary School
San Rafael, California

Lois Wendt
Teacher
Crystal Heights School
Crystal, Minnesota

ODYSSEY
An HBJ Literature Program, Levels 1-8

odyssey (äd′ ə sē) *n.* A long wandering journey. Your students travel to new places, meet new characters, and discover new insights that deepen their sense of themselves and expand their view of the world…in a word, ODYSSEY. It's an adventure in memorable experiences, an introduction to the riches of the imagination.

In every level, ODYSSEY presents an exceptional variety of quality literature, written by an outstanding selection of classic and contemporary writers.

From Level 1 to Level 8, ODYSSEY will help you inspire your students to read and enjoy literature. ODYSSEY also offers students a solid foundation in literary appreciation and helps build skills in reading, writing, speaking, and listening.

Features of ODYSSEY

• High-interest poems, plays, short stories, science fiction, folk tales, excerpts from biographies and novels, essays, and more.

• Writers who represent the diversity of our society, including E.B. White, Beverly Cleary, Ernesto Galarza, Jamake Highwater, Virginia Hamilton, Laurence Yep, Nicholasa Mohr.

• Dazzling art that enhances each selection.

• A range of reading levels that will appeal to students of various reading abilities.

• A thematic structure that focuses on relationships, adventure, humor, fantasy, and more.

• Skill-building material students can use on their own.

• Student-centered activities that develop literary understanding and appreciation.

Turn the page to see samples of the features you'll find in ODYSSEY.

Here are some examples of the

From Level 1 Primer

Mix a Pancake

A poem by Christina Rossetti

Mix a pancake,
Stir a pancake,
   Pop it in the pan;
Fry the pancake,
Toss the pancake,—
   Catch it if you can.

Your students will enjoy reading the stories, plays, poems, and songs. In ODYSSEY, every student will find selections of interest and appeal.

In every book, students will read selections by award-winning authors— Maurice Sendak, Lucille Clifton, C.S. Lewis, Arnold Lobel, Karla Kuskin, E.L. Konigsburg, Langston Hughes, Taro Yashima, Natalie Babbitt, Laura Ingalls Wilder.

From Level 3

The Big Wind of '34

A tall tale by James Flora
Pictures by Marie-Louise Gay

If you stay around Grandpa long enough, you will hear all sorts of amazing stories about his farm. Some people might call them tall tales, but you can decide for yourself after reading this tale as Grandpa tells it.

When Grandma and I first came to the farm, there was no barn—just a house. We were very poor and couldn't afford to build a barn. We had a cow, and she had to sleep outside. She didn't like that at all. On cold days she would get so angry that she wouldn't give us any milk.

265

Pages reduced. Actual size 7½" x 9".

variety you'll find in ODYSSEY

Throughout ODYSSEY, your students will discover authors and illustrators whose ideas and imagery invite their readers back for more.

From Level 5

The Great Quillow

A play by Moyne Rice Smith
based on the story by James Thurber
Illustrated by Sal Murdocca

Characters

Lamplighter
Town Crier
Town Clerk
Blacksmith
Tailor
Butcher
Candymaker

Baker
Candlemaker
Cobbler
Carpenter
Locksmith
Quillow, the Toymaker
Hunder, the Giant

Setting: Village square.
Time: Many years ago.

*The village clock strikes seven.
Lamplighter enters with his long
staff and lights the street lamp.*

Hunder sits above our village
and curses it. What can we do?
He has plundered the villages
of the far countryside. And today the earth shook when he
strode onto our hillside. He

From Level 8

A Wagon Load of Bricks

A chapter from the biography *Harriet Tubman: Conductor on the
Underground Railroad* by Ann Petry
Illustrated by Kenneth Longtemps

*Harriet Tubman was a great leader in the fight against slavery
in America. Born a slave in Maryland, she ran away and made
the dangerous journey North in 1849, when she was twenty-nine.
She returned South to conduct other slaves to freedom along the
Underground Railroad. Her courage has inspired many writers,
like Ann Petry who wrote the biography from which this excerpt is
taken. Another such writer is Hildegarde Hoyt Swift, who wrote
the following verse as part of a longer poem entitled "I brought to
the New World the gift of devotion."*

*I was Harriet Tubman, who would not stay in bondage.
I followed the devious, uncharted trails to the North,
I followed the light of the North Star,
I ran away to freedom in 1849.
I was Harriet Tubman who could not stay in freedom,
While her brothers were enslaved.
. . . .
I was Harriet Tubman,
Who "never run my train off the track,
And never lost a passenger."*

FROM 1851 TO 1857, the country moved closer to civil war.
During these years Harriet Tubman made eleven trips into
Maryland to bring out slaves.

In November, 1856, she rescued Joe Bailey. In the
spring she had made two trips to the Eastern Shore.[1] The
result of one of these trips is recorded in Still's[2] "April 25¹

266

Here are more stimulating

Illustrations will help your students visualize story characters, settings, and actions, making literature a more enjoyable experience.

BANDO

From the novel *My Side of the Mountain*
by Jean Craighead George
Illustrated by Lyle Miller

It was late spring when Sam Gribley left his family's crowded New York City apartment home and set out for some land in the Catskill Mountains that his great-grandfather had once tried to farm. He carried only a penknife, a ball of string, an ax, a flint with steel,[1] and forty dollars. He knew how to fish and build fires, and he figured that was all he needed for a new life.

During his first few days in the wilds, Sam was

The Crane Maiden

A Japanese folk tale retold by Miyoko Matsutani
English version by Alvin Tresselt
Illustrated by Masami Miyamoto

Long years ago, at the edge of a small mountain village in the snow country of Japan, there lived an old man and his wife. They had little in this world that they could call their own. But they were happy in their life together.

Now one winter morning the old man set out for the village with a bundle of firewood fastened to his back. It was bitter cold. He knew he would have little trouble selling the wood. Then with the money, he would buy some food so that he and his wife could have a good supper.

As the old man trudged through the falling snow, he was suddenly aware of a fluttering sound, and a pitiful cry of *Koh, koh*. Turning from the path to investigate, he came upon a great crane frantically trying to free herself from a trap.

The old man's heart was touched with pity for the magnificent bird. While he tried to soothe the crane with tender words, his hands released the cruel spring of the trap. At once the crane flew up, joyfully calling *Koh, koh*, and disappeared into the snowy sky.

T10

93

selections from ODYSSEY

In Levels 1 and 2, wordless picture stories develop visual literacy. By reading and retelling picture stories, students increase their oral vocabulary and their ability to find meaning and "a sense of story" in pictures.

Your students will find units on fantasy, humor, and the natural world throughout the books. In Levels 5 and 8, special units focus on the people, heroes, and events in America's past. Level 7 includes a unit on myths and epics. These thematic units will help you enrich the various curriculum areas you teach.

From Level 1 Preprimer

Pages reduced. Actual size 7½" x 9"

From Level 7

ECHO & NARCISSUS

A GREEK MYTH RETOLD BY ROGER LANCELYN GREEN

ILLUSTRATED BY KATIE THAMER

The gods took a devilish delight in punishment. When someone angered one of them—and the gods were quick to take offense—the offender was tortured in a way that cleverly fit the crime. The goddess Hera, who was forever tracking down her flirtatious husband, Zeus, became particularly skilled at punishing his sweethearts. She changed one beautiful maid into a hairy bear. When Zeus tried to disguise another girl friend as a cow, Hera had a gadfly pursue the cow around the earth. Now the beautiful nymph Echo is about to feel Hera's wrath.

UP ON THE WILD, lonely mountains of Greece lived the Oreades,[1] the nymphs or fairies of the hills, and among them one of the most beautiful was called Echo. She was one of the most talkative, too, and once she talked too much and angered Hera, wife of Zeus, king of the gods.

When Zeus grew tired of the golden halls of Mount Olympus, the home of the immortal gods, he would come down to earth and wander with the nymphs on the mountains. Hera, however, was jealous and often came to see what he was doing. It seemed strange at first that she always met Echo, and that Echo kept her listening for hours on end to her stories and her gossip.

But at last Hera realized that Echo was doing this on purpose to detain her while Zeus went quietly back to Olympus as if he had never really been away.

"So nothing can stop you talking?" exclaimed Hera. "Well, Echo, I do not intend to spoil your pleasure. But from this

1. Oreades (OHR • ee • AHD • eez).

T11

Special features develop literary

Learn About Literature features help students develop an appreciation for literature and an understanding of various literary elements and devices. Students learn about such literary elements as setting, plot, and characterization. They learn to use such literary devices as rhythm, repetition, and figurative language. They become aware of illustration styles, uses of the library, and more.

Literary excerpts and examples are used to help students learn about specific aspects of literature. And activities provide opportunities for students to practice what they are learning.

Learn About

Libraries

Animals in the Library

These books are all mixed up. Some are storybooks. Some are fact books. Can you help me get the books on the right shelves?

I'll find the storybooks.

I'll find the fact books.

From Level 5

Learn About

Stories

Characters to Remember

Think about some favorite characters in stories you have read. Were they brave? determined? clever? honest? wicked? These are all *traits*. A character's traits are what make that character stand out in your mind. They are what make a character someone you are likely to remember.

A character's traits may be learned from what that character says. What traits do you detect in Beth from what she says in the following section from the story "I Never Asked for No Allergy"? In this scene, Beth is saying good-bye to her dog, Friendly, because she is allergic to him.

At the kennel I held Friendly close to me while Pa explained about the allergy to Mr. Grant. "You are welcome to swap," he said, reaching out for Friendly.

"Wait!" I said. "A person has got to say good-bye, don't they?" I looked into Friendly's eyes and wondered how I could make him understand. "I never wanted to get rid of you, Friendly. I only wanted to get rid of the aller— *Her-her-choo!*—of the allergy."

Caring, sensitive, concerned— these are traits you may have observed in Beth from what she says.

A character's traits also may be learned from what the author tells us. Here is the way author Natalie Babbitt describes Egan as he begins to climb the mountain in the story "The Megrimum."

. . . Egan was half an hour ahead by that time. And he was young and strong, alone—and determined.

Later in that story, the traits of being *strong* and *determined* are shown in what Egan does—in his actions.

Egan, deep in the mist, heard nothing. He wandered up the final stony slope toward the top like a sleepwalker lost in dreams. . . . And then he stopped, chilled suddenly out of his trance. Just ahead there came a noise as of an animal thrashing about, and the low rumble of a voice.

He crept forward, grasping the nearly forgotten stick tightly, and his heart pounded. The Megrimum! At last, the Megrimum! Slay it, perhaps—perhaps; but at least he would see it.

More thrashing in the weeds ahead. "Owanna-ooowanna," the voice seemed to murmur.

Closer and closer crept Egan and then he saw it dimly, all flailing arms, rolling about on the ground.

209

T12

understanding and appreciation

At the primary levels, *Learn About Literature* features focus on such literary elements and devices as story characters, story sequence, sound words, story structure, plots, poetry, and more.

At the intermediate levels, there are features about plays, writing quatrains (four-line poems) and limericks, figurative language, biography, characterization, and theme.

In Levels 7 and 8, these features cover a variety of topics, including writing a newspaper, performing Readers Theatre, learning about science fiction and fantasy, writing humorous essays, understanding poetry, and learning how authors use setting and point of view. There are several *Learn About Literature* features in each book at Levels 1-6, five in Level 7, and six in Level 8.

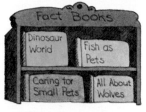

Choose a book for each animal.

1

I like dinosaurs. Where can I find out more about them?

I have a new pet ant. What can I feed her?

3

M___
hear a___
I read___

Learn About

On Stage!   **Plays**

The theater lights dim. The curtain goes up. You are about to see a play. As the actors move and speak, you find out what is happening. With the costumes and scenery, you picture the time and place.

A play is meant to be performed. That is the main difference between a play and a story. When it is written, a play *looks* different, too. It has

a cast of characters

Characters	Mrs. Brown	Paddington
	Mrs. Bird	Nurse

stage directions

(Paddington *comes in carrying a letter*.)

dialogue

Paddington: There's a letter for you, Mrs. Brown. It looks like Mr. Curry's writing.

Mrs. Brown: Yes, I'm afraid you're right.

How does a story look different from a play?

1 Does it have characters?

2 Does it have stage directions?

3 Does it have dialogue?

You will find this bear's answers below.

282

3. A story does have dialogue, but the dialogue is usually in quotation marks.

feel. This information is not in parentheses.

does tell what the characters do and how they

story does have characters, but they are not

ed at the b___

in a cast of characters

story does not have stage directions, but it

T13

ODYSSEY includes skill-building material students can do on their own

Questions and Activity pages foster students' critical reading and creative writing skills. You'll find this feature at the end of most prose selections to help you enhance the reading and writing skills you teach.

By including levels of questions that range from simple (recall and inference) to more complex (extrapolation and relating reading to experience), students may test their literal, interpretive, and critical reading skills. Activities provide opportunities for a range of responses, from speaking and writing, to drawing and performing.

In levels 7 and 8, special *Understanding Literature* sections along with the *Questions* and *Activities* add to students' knowledge and appreciation of various literary elements and techniques. The questions, activities, and composition assignments at these levels help students learn skills of self-expression, how to identify the theme of a story, explore the use of repetition for effect, create a story sequence, and more.

From Level 1 Reader

Questions

Who am I?

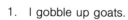

bridge

Gunniwolf

goat

Troll

1. I gobble up goats.
2. I get fat.
3. I go "trip, trap, trip, trap."
4. I am not in this story.

Activity

Here come three fat Billy Goats Gruff.

The ugly Troll has gone away.

Who waits under the bridge now?

Draw it.

Name it.

What will it say?

Questions

1. Billy made two state[...] might be fibbing. Wh[...]

2. When did Encyclope[...] had a *problem*?

3. What did Encyclope[...] to try to *solve* the p[...]

4. Why did the author [...] story, not within it?

5. In this story, a *susp[...]*
    a. is the wrongdoer[...]
    b. might be the wrongdoer.
    c. is innocent, but is accused of being the wrongdoer.

Activity

If Encyclopedia Brown had not found Sally's roller skates, he might have put an advertisement in a newspaper, offering a reward for their return. Write an advertisement for Encyclopedia. In your advertisement, tell what the skates looked like, and where and when they were last seen.

From Level 4

These special features will help your students appreciate literature even more

From Level 6

About the Author features give readers a glimpse into the lives of authors. Quotes that provide insights into the authors' ideas and techniques, and information on how authors began their careers, help students to see authors as real people.

About ISAAC BASHEVIS SINGER

Isaac Bashevis Singer's stories are set in Jewish communities much like those he knew as a young boy growing up in Poland in the early 1900s. His father was a rabbi (a leader or teacher of the Jewish religion), and his mother was a rabbi's daughter. Although he studied to become a rabbi, Isaac Bashevis Singer found work as a journalist instead. In 1935 he came to the United States and got a job on New York's *Jewish Daily Forward*, a newspaper written in Yiddish, a language spoken by many Jewish people of European background. Mr. Singer says, "When I came here, I said to my editor, 'What I want is a steady job.' He replied, 'A steady job? In a language that will die in ten years?' Yet, you see, Yiddish is still with us."

Isaac Bashevis Singer continues to write his stories in Yiddish, and then supervises their translation into English. His stories, however, have been praised for their appeal to people of all cultures. In 1979 he was given the Nobel Prize for Literature, the highest honor a writer can receive.

More Books by Isaac Bashevis Singer

Zlateh the Goat and Other Stories
The Fearsome Inn
A Day of Pleasure: Stories of a Boy Growing Up in Warsaw

From Level 4

BOOKSHELF

The Ghost on Saturday Night by Sid Fleischman. Little, Brown, 1974. Opie guides a mean-looking stranger through the thick fog. His reward is two tickets to a ghost-raising. Opie doesn't know he has front-row seats to a bank robbery, too.

The Trouble with Jenny's Ear by Oliver Butterworth. Little, Brown, 1960. When Jenny hears thoughts before they are spoken, she begins to wonder what is wrong with her.

Katie John by Mary Calhoun. Harper & Row, 1960. Katie John thinks she is going to spend a boring summer in Missouri. Then a neighbor tells her that the house Katie is staying in is haunted.

A-Haunting We Will Go; Ghostly Stories and Poems collected by Lee Bennett Hopkins. Albert Whitman, 1977. Some of these ghost stories and poems will make you laugh. Some will make you shiver.

The Shrinking of Treehorn by Florence Parry Heide. Holiday House, 1971. Treehorn sees that shelves are getting higher, and his clothes are getting looser. Can he really be shrinking?

119

At the end of each textbook, Levels 4-8, definitions of important words provide independent vocabulary study.

A list of key literary terms appears at the end of each textbook, Levels 6-8. Definitions as well as examples taken from the selections help to explain the meaning and use of each literary element or device.

To encourage independent reading, *Bookshelf* provides an annotated list of books that students may read on their own for enjoyment and for further study of each unit theme. This feature appears at the end of each unit in Levels 2-8.

Annotated Teacher's Editions

Teacher's Editions provide you with all the material you need to teach each lesson: objectives, pre-reading information and suggestions, post-reading discussion questions and enrichment activities. Lessons are annotated directly on the student's pages appearing in each Teacher's Edition.

From Level 2 Teacher's Edition

Most selections have at least two objectives. Some objectives focus on literary appreciation and an understanding of literature and literary elements. Other objectives show how literature relates to human experience.

Synopses provide summaries of the main points of the story or play.

The reading level of each prose selection is designated as "easy," "average," or "challenging."

Objectives ● To enjoy the humor of a play based on trickery and misunderstandings among the characters. ● To identify character traits by extending a story. ● To perform a play using Story Theater techniques.
Synopsis of the Play A donkey, a dog, a cat, and a rooster travel to Bremen to become musicians. During their journey they discover three robbers feasting inside a house. The hungry animals give a screeching musical concert to frighten the robbers away from their meal. Later that night one of the robbers enters the house, only to be ambushed by the animals. Thinking that goblins are haunting the house, the robbers run away for good.

The Traveling Musicians

Reading Level Challenging

218

Pages reduced. Actual size 7½" x 9".

Where appropriate, a background section provides such useful information as historical or geographical details, cultural or ethnic background, and awards won by the book or author.

Introductory material often sets the mood of each selection or relates the subject or theme to something familiar to students, establishing a purpose for reading each selection.

Key vocabulary words needed for students to understand the selection are listed. Page numbers identify the location where each word first appears.

Introducing the Play *As long as there have been people, there have been folk tales. Folk tales were not written down at first, but were told and retold as stories throughout the years. During the 1800s, Jacob and Wilhelm Grimm collected many of the German folk tales that they had heard. One of these is* The Traveling Musicians, *a story about four friends who want to be musicians.*

Word to Know
musicians (myōō·zish′·ənz): performers or composers of music. (Point to the word in the title.)

Characters

Storyteller 1	**Dog**	**Robber 1**
Storyteller 2	**Rooster**	**Robber 2**
Donkey	**Cat**	**Robber 3**

Storyteller 1: Once there was a donkey who had worked for his master for many years. At last he grew too old to carry wheat to the mill. His master did not want him any more.

Donkey: My body is weak, but my voice is still strong. I think I will go to the town of Bremen and sing for my living.

Pronounced /brem′·ən/. Bremen is a port city in northwestern Germany.

Brief marginal notes provide pronunciations and definitions of words and clarify and highlight portions of the text.

Storyteller 2: So the donkey ran away. On the way to Bremen he met a dog. She was lying by the side of the road panting.

219

Lesson continued on next page. ▶

Discussion Questions encourage students to interpret and apply what they have read.

Optional group and individual activities encourage a wide range of student response through composition, oral interpretation, dramatization, art, and other forms of expression.

Discussion Question *When the robber returned to the house, each animal did something to frighten him away. How could a goat, a pig, a cow, and a kangaroo have frightened the robber?* (Possible answers: a goat could butt; a pig could grunt; a cow could bite; a kangaroo could box.)

Enriching Activities **1.** *Story Theater.* Have the children perform the play using Story Theater techniques. Some children might read the parts of the storytellers and the characters while others pantomime the characters' actions. See the front of this book for Story Theater techniques. **2.** *Music.* Ask the children to mimic the sounds of different animals. Then have them combine their sounds in an animal chorus.

Questions

1. Who were the four musicians?

2. One robber saw two lights. What were the lights?

3. The robber said he heard a goblin shout, "Cook him in a stew." What was *really* said?

4. What do you think is the funniest part of this play?

1. Literal/recall The dog; the cat; the donkey; the rooster. (page 219)
2. Interpretive/ inference The cat's eyes. (page 228)
3. Literal/recall "Cock-a-doodle-doo-o!" (page 229)
4. Critical/relating to experience This question is open to personal opinion, so expect different answers from the children.

Answers to the questions in the student's book are given on the same page as the student questions. Page numbers provide references for re-reading.

Each question is identified by two labels (e.g., literal/recall). The first label refers to the type of reading skill students must use to answer the question. The second label identifies the type of question being asked.

Activity

The four friends in the story lived together and shared the work. Tell what job each one did. Draw a picture or write one sentence about each animal.

Interpretive/ extrapolation *Drawing/writing.* Encourage the children to recall the natural abilities of each animal, but do not discourage imaginative answers.

231

A special guide for the teacher

"Teaching Literature in the Classroom" is a special guide for the teacher who wants to enrich and extend students' reading of literature. It includes suggestions for such activities as dramatization, writing, language, and art projects.

From Levels 1-8 Teacher's Editions

Teaching Literature in the Classroom *Sam Leaton Sebesta*

> I hear, and I forget.
> I see, and I remember.
> I do, and I understand.
>
> Chinese proverb

A S TEACHERS, we want children and young people to discover the joy of reading literature. With this discovery, they become free to pursue this pleasure independently, now and throughout their lifetimes. But we want something more for the young people we teach. We want them to be able to read literature not only with pleasure, but also with understanding. We want them to be able to respond thoughtfully to their reading—to *interact* with it—so that both their pleasure and their knowledge are increased.

Students' interaction with literature begins with teachers who approach literature with joy and excitement. Once a teacher shares this enthusiasm with students, the stage is set for their own interaction with literature, which can be as multifaceted as the teacher and the students wish to make it. This interaction can also be fostered by a good literature program that offers teachers both depth and breadth of selection, as well as providing a structure for helping students to understand and appreciate literature.

Good literary instruction proceeds in a two-phase cycle. First, reading a good selection motivates students to respond expressively to what they have read. Second, proper guidance of their responses enables students to build knowledge and skills that help them understand the next selection they encounter. The goal of such a process is students' continued reading and increasing enjoyment of literature.

The following discussion will provide a number of general guidelines as well as practical ideas for using literature in the classroom. The ideas are divided into four sections, beginning with the reading experience and discussion of literature and then considering other responses to literature—oral and written composition, interpretive reading and dramatization, and the arts. Methodological questions are raised and answered as each section and its activities are developed. Many suggestions for activities are also included throughout the lessons in this Teacher's Edition.

The Reading Experience

PREPARING FOR READING

For beginning readers, the first reading of a poem or a story is a shared experience, with the teacher reading aloud and the students joining in on a refrain or a predictable passage. Beyond this stage, students can be expected to read selections independently, but guidance and motivation are still important. The Teacher's Editions for this program offer suggestions for such guided preparation for reading: questions to raise

T30

Introduction to ODYSSEY

Tell me, Muse, of the man of many ways, who was driven
far journeys, after he had sacked Troy's sacred citadel.
Many were they whose cities he saw, whose minds he learned of,
many the pains he suffered in his spirit on the wide sea,
struggling for his own life and the homecoming of his companions.
. . . .
. . . Goddess, daughter of Zeus, speak, and begin our story.

The Odyssey of Homer

THE "MAN OF MANY WAYS" was Odysseus—king of Ithaca in ancient Greece, hero in the war against Troy, husband of Penelope, father of Telemachus, and, in all his endeavors, a man of unusual cunning and courage. Homer's great epic poem the *Odyssey* recounts Odysseus' long wandering journey home from the Trojan War. Three thousand years later, the *Odyssey* remains one of the enduring works of literature, and Odysseus, one of the enduring heroes.

When we hear the word *odyssey* today, we think of more than the epic journey of Odysseus. For as the word has become part of our language, it has taken on other meanings: a long wandering, a series of adventurous journeys marked by many changes of fortune, an intellectual or spiritual quest. In its broadest sense, we could say that odyssey describes the lifelong journey that all people undertake from birth.

It is that continuing human odyssey and our continuing wonder about it that are at the center of all literature. Though it is history that records our deeds, it is literature that seeks to express our thoughts, feelings, dreams, and wonderings about the world.

Since its origins in the chants and tales of unknown storytellers, literature has recorded events vividly, recalled our shared experience, and taught us about ourselves. In doing so, it has come to us in diverse forms—both oral and written—and in divergent voices, the sum of which is our literary heritage, drawn from the past and growing into the future.

Children's literature is one part of our literary heritage that has experienced remarkable growth in this century. With more than forty thousand children's books in print, the range of genres and content available to young people today is far greater than ever before.

While there is no lack of literature for children, however, the problem of selecting reading can be a difficult one. Some literary works meet children's interests better than others do. There are books that may be more suitable for children at a particular developmental stage or that may offer greater aesthetic growth because of their style, content, or theme. Young people need help in selecting literature that offers the best foundation both for their reading pleasure now, and for a lifetime.

In many instances, that foundation is begun at home, when parents read aloud to their children, share books with them, and talk with them about what they have read. In others, it may begin at school, when teachers and librarians read to students, encourage them to read independently, and support their spontaneous responses to reading. To a large extent, basal reading programs build on that foundation by providing a range of literature for learning and enjoyment throughout the grade levels.

In basal reading programs, however, the literature strand is only one strand in many, and the development of such basic reading skills as decoding and comprehension usually takes precedence over skills of literary appreciation and understanding. In addition, literature is often used as a vehicle to teach skills in the language arts or to enrich and extend other content areas. Despite our best efforts to provide students with a "basic education," we have often forgotten that literature is a basic subject that deserves its own place in the elementary school curriculum.

Purposes of ODYSSEY

ODYSSEY is a carefully planned program designed to provide children with a basic literary education. The program's selections and instructional material are all aimed toward its main objective: to provide a solid foundation of literary experiences on which students may build a lifetime of reading pleasure. To reach this objective, ODYSSEY has the following goals:

- To offer students a wide variety of pleasurable, independent reading of the highest literary quality
- To demonstrate the value of literature and to foster interest in reading

- To increase understanding of literature's relationship to human experience
- To develop insights into personal thoughts, feelings, and experiences
- To promote recognition of the individual's role in the community and society
- To develop an awareness of other people and cultures
- To show the power and possibilities of language as a tool for self-expression and to develop an awareness of the persuasive or manipulatory power of words
- To develop an understanding of literary forms, techniques, and styles
- To demonstrate the unique artistry of individual authors and illustrators
- To encourage thoughtful and critical responses to literature and to develop respect for the responses of others
- To develop the skills of reading comprehension, writing, and the other language arts, as well as logical thinking skills

Criteria for Selections

In choosing selections for ODYSSEY, the program's developers consulted children's literature specialists, teachers, librarians— and children and young people themselves. After potential selections were identified, program consultants (see pages T4 and T5) evaluated each selection using the following criteria:

Interest Level. Is the selection likely to interest children at this age level?

Reading Level. Will most of the children at this level be able to read the selection independently?

Quality. Does the selection have high literary quality?

Experience.   Is the selection worthwhile, either because it brings pure enjoyment to young readers or because it fosters their personal growth?

Portrayal of Ethnic, Minority, and Special Groups.   Does the selection portray all groups fairly?

Further considerations were the selections' relevance to six thematic strands and their balance in such areas as content, literary type, multicultural representation, and authorship. The final choices were made after extensive classroom testing.

Organization of ODYSSEY

The literature in ODYSSEY is organized thematically around six strands. Beginning with Reader One, the strands form the basis of six thematic units in each textbook.

STRANDS IN ODYSSEY

GROWING AND CHANGING	Roles, relationships, and personal growth
ADVENTURE AND SUSPENSE	Real and imaginary adventures
HUMOR	The humorous side of life
FANTASY	Realms of the imagination
EARTH, SEA, AND SPACE	Humans and the natural world
QUEST AND HEROISM	The many aspects of courage

The thematic strands in the program appear in the chart on pages T24 and T25.

Readability in ODYSSEY

In ODYSSEY, prose selections below grade level are usually labeled *Easy,* selections at grade level are labeled *Average,* and selections above grade level are labeled *Challenging.* The selections were evaluated on the basis of their syntactic and conceptual difficulty as well as by the appropriate readability formula.

Level One.   Because most first-grade children are not independent readers, the selections in the three textbooks at Level One are intended for teacher-directed reading and for shared reading experiences. For example, the teacher might begin by reading aloud a selection such as a poem with a refrain or a story with repetition or predictable "next sentences." The teacher can then invite the class to "take the next part" or to read aloud in unison. Simple plays—usually presented in the Readers Theatre format—provide still more opportunities for shared reading experiences. To promote oral language development, the Level One readers include content-rich pictures and wordless picture stories so that children may tell or write the story they "read" in the illustrations. Some easy stories, which are labeled as such in the Teacher's Editions, can be read independently by able readers.

Levels Two through Eight.   At Levels Two and Three, most prose selections meet the reading abilities of average and above-average readers, with the majority of the selections falling within the average range, as determined mainly by the Spache readability formula. At Levels Four through Eight, most selections continue to meet the reading abilities of the average reader, with the range of reading levels widening to include more selections for below-average and gifted readers. Readability of Levels Four through Eight has been determined mainly by the Dale-Chall readability formula. Since the Dale-Chall readability level of much adult literature is seventh- to eighth-grade, however, in Levels Seven and Eight the label *Challenging* means at or above seventh-grade level; *Average,* sixth grade; *Easy,* fifth grade and below.

Evaluation in the Program

In evaluating the program's success in the classroom, the central question should be whether the selections have enhanced the students' enjoyment of literature. This is an affective outcome that no written test can assess, but teachers can assess progress informally, asking students for their opinions about the literature; listening to their spontaneous comments, especially their expressions of interest in reading and literature; and observing whether they seek out further literary experiences. Brief anecdotal records of the students' responses will provide valid and direct evidence that the program's goal is being met.

The questions and activities in the program can be used to evaluate the students' knowledge of literary elements and techniques, and their growth in literary appreciation, reading comprehension, and both oral and written composition. Questions at the literal level will yield brief yet adequate information on students' abilities in literal comprehension. Questions at the interpretive level can provide information about students' abilities to make inferences, to express opinions based on their reading, and to substantiate both kinds of responses. Questions that require critical thinking skills can assess students' abilities to read "beyond the lines," that is, to integrate what they have read with their own experience or to apply it in a different context. Even though their answers to critical-level questions are subjective and thus will vary greatly, the students' responses can be evaluated in terms of their fluency, flexibility, elaboration, originality, and logic.

Literature for a Lifetime

A literature program for children requires faith in the lasting effects of teaching and learning. Such faith seems warranted. Most adults who like to read literature can describe one or a hundred rewarding contacts with books in childhood and adolescence. Many such readers might identify with Francie, the child in Betty Smith's novel *A Tree Grows in Brooklyn,* who realizes suddenly the benefits of having learned to read:

> From that time on, the world was hers for the reading. She would never be lonely again, never miss the lack of intimate friends. Books became her friends and there was one for every mood. There was poetry for quiet companionship. There was adventure when she tired of quiet hours. There would be love stories when she came into adolescence and when she wanted to feel a closeness to someone she could read a biography. On that day when she first knew she could read, she made a vow to read one book a day as long as she lived.

The journeys children take through books can carry them as near as a city street or as far away as a dragon's lair; but wherever their reading leads them, the discovery of literature in childhood can extend and enrich their lives far beyond that time. In books readers may live more lives, try on more costumes, step into more situations than any one life could possibly afford. ODYSSEY is just the beginning of that life-long journey through literature.

Thematic Strands in ODYSSEY

Level	GROWING AND CHANGING	ADVENTURE AND SUSPENSE	HUMOR
1*	**Let's Go Together** Relationships with friends and family	**Far, Far Away** The call of adventure	**What a Surprise!** Humorous experiences with an element of surprise
2	**We Could Be Friends** The many aspects of friendship	**Something Is There** Mysterious happenings	**Tell Me Something Very Silly** Comical characters; improbable occurrences
3	**Good Times** Building relationships	**You Can't Catch Me** Ingenious escapes from danger	**It's Not Funny** Humorous predicaments
4	**When Paths Cross** Contrasting points of view	**Across the Land and Sea** Journeys to new lands	**What a Character!** Remarkable characters in humorous situations
5	**Never Give Up** The role of perseverance in personal growth	**Facing the Unknown** Suspenseful encounters in different settings	**It Must Be a Trick** Tricksters and trickery
6	**Dream Keepers** Recognizing individual identity and talents	**Expect the Unexpected** Unexpected encounters and surprise endings	**Funny Side Up** Mix-ups, mishaps, and misunderstandings
7	**Reflections** Experiences leading to personal growth and life changes	**On a Moonless Night** Strange occurrences	**Monkey Business** The techniques of humor
8	**Spectrum** The many paths to self-knowledge and maturity	**Only Darkness Ticking** The techniques of suspense	**On the Funny Side** Humor in ordinary and extraordinary situations

★Refers only to Level 1 Reader. Strands are not grouped by units in Preprimer and Primer.

FANTASY	EARTH, SEA, AND SPACE	QUEST AND HEROISM
Tell Me a Story Adventures of fantasy characters	**I Wonder** The wonders of nature	**I'm Growing** Awareness of physical growth
Long, Long Ago Magical beings, places, and things	**Animals All Around** Animals and their environments	**I Can Do It!** Acting independently and assuming new roles
Would You Believe It! Tall tales	**There Is a Season . . .** The cycle of the seasons	**Tell Me the Name** Awareness of personal identity
When the Moon Shines Illusions and transformations	**To Live with Animals** Relationships between animals and humans	**Problems and Puzzles** Meeting challenges and solving problems
Truly Amazing Talents Characters with amazing or unusual talents	**To Live with Nature** Living with the creatures and forces of nature; survival	**From America's Past** Characters and events from American history
Time Travelers Exploring time through fantasy	**A Tree of Ice, A Rain of Stars** Nature as a source of inspiration and beliefs	**Tests of Courage** The many forms of courage in myth, legend, and contemporary life
A Gift of Story Greek myths and epic heroes	**Voices from the Earth** Encounters with animals and elements in nature	**To Stand Alone** Individual courage in the face of adversity
Another Where, Another When The elements and varieties of fantasy	**Secrets** The interrelationship of humans and nature	**We, the People** The importance of ordinary people in American history

Skills Index for Level Two

This Skills Index will help you to locate the pages on which each listed skill is presented in a level of ODYSSEY: AN HBJ LITERATURE PROGRAM. Boldfaced page references indicate that the skill is presented in the pupil's textbook. Other references are to teaching suggestions and activities in the teacher's edition.

    The numbers preceding the items in the index correspond to the HBJ Skills Code. This code may be used to correlate skills in ODYSSEY with other language arts and reading programs published after 1980 by Harcourt Brace Jovanovich. Teachers who wish to cross-reference these programs may do so by referring to these same numbers that appear in other programs. The index can also serve as a basis for correlating ODYSSEY with the management system or curriculum guide used in your school.

Skills Code Number	SKILL	PAGES
	COMPREHENSION	
3.1	**To Identify and Use Context Clues**	
3.1.4	to relate reading to experience	12, 15, 43, **54,** 75, 77, 101, 117, 125, 144, 145, 155, 166, 205, 211, 212, **231,** 235, 241, 242, 255
3.2	**To Classify**	
3.2.1	to classify by common attributes or association	145, 172–173, 181, 216
3.3	**To Identify and Use Literal Comprehension Skills**	
3.3.1	to find or recall specific details	12, **31,** 37, **43, 75,** 77, 94, 99, **117,** 118, 123, **141,** 145, 152, **165,** 169, **181,** 184, 188, **201,** 201, 202, **211,** 212, 216, **231,** 232–233, **233, 240,** 240, **253,** 253
3.3.3	to identify stated cause and effect relationships	**31, 75, 182–184,** 182–184, **211, 240**
3.3.6.4	to state information in different words	123, 166
3.3.7	to recognize sequence	39, 78–93, 233
3.3.7.1	to recognize or interpret time order	39, 233
3.3.7.3	to recognize a sequence of pictures	**78–93**

Activities Index

Teaching Literature in the Classroom
Sam Leaton Sebesta

I hear, and I forget.
I see, and I remember.
I do, and I understand.

Chinese proverb

AS TEACHERS, we want children and young people to discover the joy of reading literature. With this discovery, they become free to pursue this pleasure independently, now and throughout their lifetimes. But we want something more for the young people we teach. We want them to be able to read literature not only with pleasure, but also with understanding. We want them to be able to respond thoughtfully to their reading—to *interact* with it—so that both their pleasure and their knowledge are increased.

Students' interaction with literature begins with teachers who approach literature with joy and excitement. Once a teacher shares this enthusiasm with students, the stage is set for their own interaction with literature, which can be as multifaceted as the teacher and the students wish to make it. This interaction can also be fostered by a good literature program that offers teachers both depth and breadth of selection, as well as providing a structure for helping students to understand and appreciate literature.

Good literary instruction proceeds in a two-phase cycle. First, reading a good selection motivates students to respond expressively to what they have read. Second, proper guidance of their responses enables students to build knowledge and skills that help them understand the next selection they encounter. The goal of such a process is students' continued reading and increasing enjoyment of literature.

The following discussion will provide a number of general guidelines as well as practical ideas for using literature in the classroom. The ideas are divided into four sections, beginning with the reading experience and discussion of literature and then considering other responses to literature—oral and written composition, interpretive reading and dramatization, and the arts. Methodological questions are raised and answered as each section and its activities are developed. Many suggestions for activities are also included throughout the lessons in this Teacher's Edition.

The Reading Experience

PREPARING FOR READING

For beginning readers, the first reading of a poem or a story is a shared experience, with the teacher reading aloud and the students joining in on a refrain or a predictable passage. Beyond this stage, students can be expected to read selections independently, but guidance and motivation are still important. The Teacher's Editions for this program offer suggestions for such guided preparation for reading: questions to raise before the reading takes place; brief comments about the work that is to be read; and *definitions* of key terms to help students understand the selection.

Preparation may require only a few moments, but it is useful for several reasons. It allows students to begin reading with a "warmed-up motor," prepared to respond to the selection. It helps students establish a focus for reading. And it helps remove the barriers that unfamiliar words may otherwise present. Research has shown that preteaching relevant vocabulary increases student comprehension.

SILENT AND ORAL READING

Most reading specialists recommend that first readings always be silent, independent readings. They point out that silent reading permits each student to read at his or her own pace. It also encourages reflection and allows both time for response and the chance to go back and *reread* a passage before going on. Initial silent reading helps students enjoy and interpret a selection further during a later oral reading.

This recommendation for silent reading first has exceptions. Most poems should be read aloud initially. Anecdotes and funny stories beg for sharing and may lose their appeal if assigned to be read silently. When the language or theme of a selection is complex, guided oral reading helps students share the literary experience from the start.

At no time, however, should oral reading be considered a mere exercise in "getting all the words right." Rather, it is a means to guiding understanding. Most often, this guidance is better done by (1) *preparing students to read silently*, (2) *encouraging silent reading according to each student's rate and reading strategies*, and (3) *later having students reread all or part of a selection for a purpose—to support a point, to share an enthusiasm, or to enliven a work through oral interpretation.*

DISCUSSING A SELECTION

Once a selection is read, discussion can enhance the literary experience. The main purpose of such discussion is to allow students to speak, to express their responses to the literature they are reading, and to listen to the varied responses of their classmates. In addition, discussion can be an informal way for you to assess students' enjoyment, involvement, and understanding of what they have read. Asking a general opening question and inviting students to ask questions are good ways to begin a discussion that leads to more structured questions and activities.

Opening discussion should be nonthreatening. It should invite immediate, pertinent response. It should, if possible, set the stage for more focused questions and activities. Here are three effective ways to begin a discussion. (Consult each selection in the Teacher's Edition for specific suggestions.)

1. *Ask what students discovered as a result of their reading.* Sometimes this may be a focusing question, based on a preparation question posed before the reading. Sometimes the question can be a more general opener—"Tell me about the story"—that invites students to share their responses, fresh from reading, without imposing a structure.

2. *Refer to the question-and-activity page in the pupil's textbook*, which is included after most of the longer prose selections. Students who have prepared responses to items on the page will have something to contribute at once, and discussion will get off to a good start.

3. *Ask each student to find one passage in the story that is exciting to read aloud—* a segment that might entice a listener to read the entire story. Subsequent discussion can begin with a request for justification: "Why did you choose that part?"

Early in the discussion, invite student questions: "What did you wonder about as you read the story? Did a question come to your mind as you read this poem?" Such a procedure encourages self-generated questioning as one reads, a basic strategy that good readers use constantly.

Inquiry Within the Program. In ODYSSEY, a variety of questions help teachers focus and extend discussions about literature, and also help provide well-rounded, unified lessons. Some of the questions are derived from objectives stated in the teaching notes preceding each selection. Others review objectives from earlier readings or seek to broaden the lesson. In each case, questions pertain to the central meaning and significance of the work, their chief purpose being to enhance students' enjoyment and understanding and to allow them to use their listening, speaking, and writing skills when responding.

The following are the five types of questions used in the ODYSSEY program:

1. **Recall** *questions ask the student to specify information, or data, present in the story, poem, or nonfiction selection.* Students are not asked to recall random facts, but information derived from the focus of the selection. Often this information is used in subsequent higher-level discussion. With some students, the recall level needs little attention. With others, you may need to elicit additional recall, such as sequence of events, before proceeding to discuss a selection above the literal level.

2. **Inference** *questions are based on the information given in a selection, but they require more than simple recall.* Inference questions require conjectures from the student based on knowledge of the selection's content, on personal experience, and on imagination. The author of a story, for example, may present three details, three "facts" about the setting from which the reader is expected to infer additional details. Many readers do this automatically, but some do not. Inference questions, then, give practice and encouragement in figuring out what happened between events described in a story, in determining whose point of view is presented in a poem, or in speculating about cause and effect when the relationship is implied rather than directly described. This type of question recognizes that no literary work *tells* all. Rather, every literary work *suggests*, and the reader interacts by inferring the missing parts. Much of the fun of reading literature comes from inference.

3. **Extrapolation** *questions, extensions of inference, invite the reader to consider, for example, what happened* after *the story ended, how a character might act in another situation, or what the speaker of a poem might say about an object or scene other than that described in the poem.* (To extrapolate means "to project, extend or expand something that is known into an unknown area; to conjecture.") Extrapolation questions are often more extensive and more speculative than inference questions, and they may extend creative thinking toward writing, drawing, or speaking.[1]

4. **Relating reading to experience** *questions, as the term is used here, are those questions that invite the reader to relate the literary work directly to his or her own life.* The basic form for this question is "How is your own experience *like* some-

---

1. Robert A. Collins, "Extrapolation: Going Beyond the Present," *Media and Methods*, 16, no. 3 (November 1979); 22–25.

thing in the selection you have just read?"
A variation is "Based on your experience,
what would you have done in the situation
described in this selection?" Throughout
the program, this basic idea is varied to
meet the specifics of a story, a poem, or a
work of nonfiction.

5. **Language and vocabulary** *questions are closed-answer items to check a
reader's knowledge of key terms, idioms, or
stylistic features.* A part of literary awareness resides in understanding what words
mean as well as in understanding nuances
of style.

As explained on page T18 of this textbook, each question and activity in the
ODYSSEY program also has a label identifying the reading skill students will use
when responding. These skills are **literal**,
interpretive, and **critical thinking**.

Using Questions to Teach.   The question types described above are used in
ODYSSEY mainly for teaching purposes,
not testing. Most questions can start a
series of responses, and one question may
lead to another without interrupting the
main topic of discussion. The resulting
pattern of discussion may not be question–
answer, question–answer, as it is likely to
be in testing. Instead, the pattern for the
discussion of a story may be the following:
a question asking for clarification of a word
or phrase leads to a question involving
recall of the story events, which in turn
leads to a question asking for an interpretation of a character's reaction to those
events.

Try applying some of the following strategies during your classroom discussions:

1. *Probing.* A probe can be a request for
additional information to clarify or elaborate
on a response, or it can be a request for
other answers. Such questions as "Any
other ideas?" or "Can you tell us *more*

about that idea?" can develop a discussion
without fragmenting it. Listen to a response
and decide whether a probe is needed.

2. *Requesting verification.* Ask students
to return to the text in order to verify a point.
Students may be asked to substantiate
opinions as well as locate bases for state-
ments of fact. At other times students
may be called upon to use other sources,
including their own experience, to verify a
statement.

3. *Providing wait time.* The *wait time*, or
think time, principle simply means that a
time of silence comes between a question
and a response.[2] Research shows that
classes using wait time have better discussions. Responses are longer, and students
show higher-level thinking than when the
wait time principle is ignored.

To apply this strategy, you might begin
by saying, "Now I'm going to ask you a
very thought-provoking question. Take time
to think about it before you tell us what you
think." Ask the question, and then allow
several seconds to elapse before calling for
a response. *After* hearing a response, wait
several seconds before commenting or
asking for other responses.

EVALUATING READING EXPERIENCES

To evaluate whether your literature discussions, along with pre-reading preparation
and silent, independent reading, are of benefit to the students, observe students on the
following:

1. *Notice whether students seem to seek
new reading experiences and whether literature lessons are eagerly anticipated.* If

---

2. Linda B. Gambrell, "Think-Time: Implications for
Reading Instruction," *The Reading Teacher*, 34, no. 2
(November 1980); 143–146.

these reactions occur, the students are attaining the goals of the reading experience, including pleasure, insight into human behavior, and appreciation for language and style.

2. *Consider students' responses during discussions*. Do they enter discussions enthusiastically? Do all contribute? Is there a give-and-take during the discussions that seems to produce a deepened understanding of the selection? (The importance of building enthusiasm should not be underestimated. Each new reading experience enjoyed by a child makes it less likely that he or she will become a nonreader.)

3. *Consider students' answers to the questions themselves, in order to identify their level of reading comprehension*. The literal level items (recall, vocabulary) are usually easy to evaluate since they call for *convergent* thinking. This means that students will come to an agreement on a "right answer." Though suggested "right answers" are provided in the Teacher's Edition, students' answers may vary and still be "right."

Above-literal items (inference, extrapolation, relating reading to experience) seek to develop *divergent* thinking. This means that students' answers will be different from one another since they are based on individual opinion and experience. Although examples of responses are presented in the Teacher's Editions and labeled "Possible answer(s)," no one can predict the range of responses that can arise from divergent thinking. The following criteria can be used, however, in evaluating such responses:

- *Fluency*. Do students contribute easily to the discussion? Are they able to produce many responses?
- *Flexibility*. Are responses varied so that several *different* ideas are contributed?
- *Originality*. Are some students' responses creative as well as appropriate to

the question; that is, do some students demonstrate a unique ability to discern and to solve the problems posed by the question?
- *Elaboration*. When probed, can students expand their responses by adding details?

4. *Observe the students' responses to the reading through activities such as oral or written composition, dramatization, or creative expression in the arts*. If the reading experience and discussion are indeed promoting students' responses to literature, activities will help reveal and develop such responses.

Additional Readings

Torrance, E. Paul, and Myers, R. E., *Creative Learning and Teaching*. New York: Dodd, Mead, 1970. Chapters 7 through 10 contain suggestions for asking good divergent-thinking questions, with factors to consider in evaluating responses.

Carin, Arthur A., and Sund, Robert B., *Developing Questioning Techniques: A Self-Concept Approach*. New York: Charles E. Merrill, 1971. The entire book contains helpful, practical suggestions for making discussion sessions popular and meaningful.

Sebesta, Sam Leaton, and Iverson, William J., *Literature for Thursday's Child*. Chicago: Science Research Associates, 1975. Part III contains a plan for integrating questions and activities of different types and levels.

Ruddell, Robert B., *Reading-Language Instruction: Innovative Practices*. Englewood Cliffs, N.J.: Prentice Hall, 1974. Chapter 11 includes transcripts and a guide to developing questioning strategies and promoting verbal interaction.

Oral and Written Composition

FROM RESPONSE TO COMPOSITION

Children and young people have much to say. They enjoy talking about what they have read. Their enthusiasm goes beyond the act of reading and answering a few questions about a literary selection.

Young readers may enjoy *retelling* a story, thus transforming the written form into oral language. They are likely to add a phrase here, change a word there, or *infer* a scrap of conversation or a detail of setting. Such alterations may not indicate a faulty memory at all, but rather show the teller's ability to reconstruct literature in imagination. Young readers may *extrapolate* from, or extend, a story. They may tell what might have happened after the story ended, or how it might have been different in another setting or situation. They may also relate the selection to their own experience, and thus *interpret* its meaning in terms of their own lives.

All of these types of responses have appeared in the oral and written responses of children and young people as they reacted to literature.[3,4] When such responses comprise a group of sentences with a central topic or purpose, they become a *composition*. A composition may be oral or written. It may be the product of an entire class, as when students dictate a paragraph to the teacher. It may be the product of a pair of students working together to stimulate each other's ideas and to share the speaking or writing task. A composition may also be done by an individual who either writes it down or dictates it into a tape recorder or to another person.

Preparing for Composition. The preparation process for composition should begin orally, even if the result is to be a written product. An oral warm-up stimulates ideas through interaction. It permits immediate feedback and the chance to try out an idea before taking the effort and time to shape it completely.

At first, during the oral warm-up, students may use brainstorming techniques. Working in pairs or small groups, they are encouraged to say anything that comes to mind relevant to the assignment. Later in the warm-up, they review and evaluate what has been said.

It is good to remember, however, that some students work better alone during the warm-up time. These students need a period of quiet time to work uninterrupted on their ideas.

Where and When to Write. The time and place for composition may vary according to your needs and those of your students. A writing corner, partially separated from the rest of the classroom, helps give some children inspiration and privacy for their task. Others are quite happy to remain with the group, perhaps gaining confidence through numbers. Some sit "properly" at their desks while others may capture the flow of ideas in a more informal, relaxed posture.

Some teachers like to assign a composition project, encourage warm-up for fluency, and then set the entire class to the oral or written composition task. While stu-

---

3. Alan C. Purves with Victoria Rippere, *Elements of Writing About a Literary Work: A Study of Response to Literature* (Urbana, Illinois: National Council of Teachers of English, 1968).

4. James R. Squire, *The Responses of Adolescents While Reading Four Short Stories* (Urbana, Illinois: National Council of Teachers of English, 1964).

dents work, the teacher circulates about the room offering individual help.

Other teachers make composition an on-going process. Students may work on the assigned task at almost any time in the day. This plan has the advantage of permitting children to seize the moment of inspiration and work on an independent schedule. Its results are excitingly described in a classic book about creative composition, *They All Want To Write*, by Alvina Treut Burrows and three other teachers who experimented with the plan over a period of four years.[5]

THE ORAL COMPOSITION PROCESS

In the primary grades, oral composition is often spontaneous. For example, suppose a second-grade class had just read James Marshall's humorous story "Split Pea Soup," in which George is faced with eating his least favorite food every time he visits his friend Martha. The teacher may prepare the class for a composition assignment with a question such as, "What do you think Martha did the next time George came to visit her?" After inviting a number of answers, the teacher may suggest that the group compose a story about George's next visit. The group decides on one of the answers gathered from the discussion as story material.

Now the oral story process begins. If oral composition is a new experience, you and the group may be satisfied with a few sentences describing the chosen incident. There is no "editing" and no rejection of ideas. It is more important to get each group member to contribute something to the story. As a follow-up, some children

may perform the story as a puppet show (see page T41) while others illustrate the story.

Refining the Story. Gradually these spontaneous story-making sessions can be modified and enriched. After the warm-up, two or three children can choose one of the story ideas and prepare to tell it before the group. Alternatively, the entire class can continue to work on a story, but this time you might add some oral editing skillfully and unobtrusively.

Suppose, for example, that the group has just read "The Garden," one of Arnold Lobel's Frog and Toad stories (Level Two). Now the group is composing a story about what happens after Toad's seeds begin to grow in his garden. A main happening has been agreed upon: the seeds will grow into such large flowers that Toad's house will be covered. One child suggests as a first sentence for the story, "The flowers got so big that Toad couldn't find his house when he came home from the store."

Now the teacher can help extend and refine the story, "Why had Toad gone to the store in the first place?"

Student 1: He went to buy a watering can.
Student 2: He bought some fast-grow pills he saw on television.
Student 3: A dog on TV said, "Give your flowers a treat with Quick Grow!"
Teacher: Now let's go back and start the story.
Student 1: Next day, Toad went to the store. He bought some pills to make his flowers grow. Then he bought a watering can.
Student 4: When he came back, he said, "Where's my house? All I can see is flowers!"
Student 3: A flower said, "Get out of here! I need that place where you are so I can grow."

5. Alvina Treut Burrows, et al. *They All Want to Write: Written English in the Elementary Schools,* 3d ed. (New York: Holt, Rinehart & Winston, 1964).

Teacher: What did the flower look like—the one that said that?

Student 3: It was pink and it had a big tongue hanging out. . . .

As the story continues, the teacher can ask questions to help students organize and amplify it. There must be a give-and-take: encouragement to take risks, to try out ideas, and to alter the story when a "better" way is discovered.

THE WRITTEN COMPOSITION

If the story is deemed a success by its makers, the oral composition may merge into writing. In the primary grades, the teacher may write the story on the chalkboard or on a large note pad or a sheet of newsprint as the students watch. Later the story can be copied onto a ditto master and duplicated. Each student can receive a copy to illustrate or to practice reading aloud.

Writing a First Draft. The oral composition may also be transcribed by the students themselves. Many children move early toward independence in writing skills so that, after the initial warm-up, they can proceed on their own. Here, as in earlier stages, encourage risk taking and trial and error.

It is best *not* to ask that the first draft of a story, a poem, or a nonfiction composition be a finished product. Instead suggest that students begin writing by simply "filling a page" with attempts to start the composition in an interesting manner, with thoughts that need to be jotted down lest they be forgotten in the final writing, or with scraps of conversation or detail. Then, instruct students to prepare the first draft by writing on every other line, so that revisions can be made using the empty in-between lines.

Students should be free to scratch out and scribble in; they should be encouraged to attempt spelling words that they want to use, whether they can spell them correctly or not. Such use of "invented spellings" helps students achieve fluency and leaves them free to concentrate on expressing their ideas. Neatness and correctness are reserved for the final draft.

EDITING THE COMPOSITION

The trial and error of the composition process is a form of editing. When a first draft of a composition, oral or written, is planned and then reviewed for practice and improvement, editing is taking place.

Editing needs to be taught—and taught gradually. It is self-criticism, but criticism with a constructive purpose: to go over one's original creation with a listener's ear or a reader's eye to figure out how the creation can be improved. Editing is not correcting. It is reshaping, deciding whether a scene in a story ought to be changed in some way or whether a paragraph in a report belongs somewhere else. It is revising sentences and words that lack force or fail to say what is intended. For example, the teacher who asked the student to describe the flower in the discussion about Toad's garden was helping the child expand, and hence edit, his or her first oral draft. The child's original version, "A flower said, 'Get out of here!'" might therefore become "A big pink flower stuck its tongue out and said, 'Get out of here!'"

Developing Editing Skills at Intermediate and Upper Grades. At the intermediate grade levels and above, the skills of editing may be more directly taught. A series of questions like the following, organized by category, can be used according to what is to be stressed in a lesson.

Editing Story Structure.
- Does your story start at an exciting place?
- Would a certain scene be more interesting if you expanded it?
- Is there a scene that is too long?
- Would some of the story be lost if the scene were shortened?

Editing Conversation.
- Does the dialogue "sound" like spoken language?
- Is there conversation in your story that is just "filler" and could be left out?
- Is there a place where conversation needs to be added to increase suspense or to move the story along?

Editing Sentences.
- Is there a place in your story where you can help your composition flow by using one of these connector words or phrases: *so*, *therefore*, *if—then*, *because*, *since*?
- Can one sentence be combined with another to make the meaning clearer? (Note: Language arts textbooks provide sequences and practice in sentence *combining* and *expanding*. The emphasis in editing may be placed on the specific skills concurrently taught in the language arts text used in the class.)

Editing Words.
- Can you make your writing style more direct by striking out empty words such as *very* and *a lot*?
- Can you use a more specific descriptive term by finding a synonym in a thesaurus?

At upper grade levels, students may be introduced to proofreaders' marks such as those used for deletion, insertion, and new paragraph, along with the term *stet*, which means "do not make the change indicated." These aids to editing are in most dictionaries.

Correcting for a Final Draft. To insist that everything spoken or written be perfect in mechanics can be stultifying, yet correct spelling, punctuation, capitalization, paragraphing, and all the other rudiments of acceptable form must be taught.

The best way to teach mechanics without hampering fluency is to distinguish between *process* and *product*. During the composition process, emphasis should be placed upon creating—originating, exploring, and elaborating upon ideas. When the process yields a product that the student wants others to hear or read in finished form, the rules of correctness need to be followed.

Here are some helpful ways to teach mechanics:

1. *Have the students tape-record their speeches or hand in written first drafts of compositions.* You can listen to the recordings or correct the drafts, offering suggestions for improvement before the students present their work in final form.

2. *Encourage self-criticism.* Each student may be given an alphabetized list of words frequently used but sometimes misspelled. A recent source for such a list is Robert L. Hillerich's *A Writing Vocabulary of Elementary Children.*[6] A class dictionary is also a useful tool.

3. *Emphasize punctuation and handwriting when students prepare final copies of written compositions.*

Polishing the Oral Composition. Oral compositions can be practiced with the aid of a partner who acts as director. The partner may suggest changes in delivery, identifying places where pace and force may be varied, correcting pronunciation, and offering an opinion about the

6. Robert L. Hillerich, *A Writing Vocabulary of Elementary Children* (Springfield, Illinois: Charles C. Thomas, 1978).

general effect of the speech upon the audience. Directors should be cautioned, however, to make their criticisms helpful not only by pointing out what could be improved, but also by commenting on what is good about their partners' composition and the interpretation of it.

Whether students create oral or written compositions, the values of the composition process are many. Among these should be an increased appreciation both for good literature and for the skillful authors who have created it.

Additional Readings

Lewis, Claudia. *A Big Bite of the World: Children's Creative Writing.* Englewood Cliffs, N.J.: Prentice-Hall, 1979. Examples and theory of a composition program used in Bank Street College of Education and Portland State University, involving children from the ages of three through twelve.

Tiedt, Sidney W., and Tiedt, Iris M. *Language Arts Activities for the Classroom.* Boston: Allyn & Bacon, 1978. Separate chapters give numerous examples and teaching ideas for writing, spelling, and listening, as well as ideas for using poetry and fiction in the language arts program.

Stewig, John Warren. *Read to Write: Using Children's Literature as a Springboard for Teaching Writing.* 2d ed. New York: Holt, Rinehart & Winston, 1980.

Smith, James A., and Park, Dorothy M. *Word Music and Word Magic: Children's Literature Methods.* Boston: Allyn & Bacon, 1977. A wealth of examples and techniques show integration of the best in modern and classical children's literature with the entire school curriculum, including composition.

Interpretive Reading and Dramatization

INTERPRETIVE ORAL READING

Sharing Interpretations. To interpret a story or poem well requires practice and concentration. The interpretive activity should follow careful silent reading of the selection and incorporate insights gained through discussion. Interpretive oral reading usually implies an audience—one or more listeners to whom the reader presents his or her interpretation.

The key to interpretive reading is *concentration.* Readers must learn to concentrate on finding the image and the feeling they want to impart and to work steadfastly toward that goal in their oral reading. Here, then, are seven suggestions you can make to help the students in your class read aloud interpretively:

1. *Find a selection, a stanza from a poem, or a scene from a story that you really want to read aloud to others.*

2. *Figure out why you have selected it.* If it is funny, what makes it funny? The language? The action? The surprise? If it is scary, what makes it so? Frightening words? A gradual build-up to a big scare?

3. *Now visualize the images or the pictures behind the words.* If you "see" the pictures in your mind as you read the selection aloud, your listeners will see them too. Sometimes it helps to tell yourself all about the pictures you imagine. Add ideas that the author did not tell you, using your imagination as you read.

4. *If the story or poem has action, try imitating the action as you practice reading.* Then leave out the movement and try to show the action with just your voice.

5. *Practice reading until you do not have to look at the words all the time.* Then read the selection to an empty chair three meters (approximately ten feet) or more away from you. Look often at the chair as you read. If the chair were alive, could it hear you? Would it like hearing the selection the way you are reading it?

6. For intermediate and upper grades: *Identify the purpose of each scene in a story or stanza in a poem.* Write one phrase that tells that purpose, for example, *to scare*, *to surprise*, or *to win sympathy*. Then, keep that purpose in mind as you read. Write the purpose on a sign and put the sign on your practice chair. Stop in the middle of your practice reading and ask yourself, "Am I reading to show that purpose?"

7. *After you have the pictures and the purpose in mind, try experimenting with the volume and pace of your voice.* Vary your voice from almost a whisper to almost a shout, from very fast to very slow. Then use some of this variety to help your listeners get the purpose in your reading.

Improving Oral Reading. Interpretive oral reading improves with praise if the praise is specific. "You read that with a great deal of expression" is not specific enough, it does not tell the reader what he or she did effectively. A more useful comment might be "I could hear the ghost rattling the dishes when you read that scene" or "I felt the sorrow of the man and woman when the girl told them she had to leave."

Interpretive oral reading also improves with good models. Most communities contain good models, so you may want to arrange readings by amateur or professional actors, senior citizens or parents with time and talent for reading aloud. The request to "come and read to us" may bring surprising, pleasing results.

CHORAL SPEAKING

Drawing Upon the Flow and Feel of Words. "Star light, star bright, first star I've seen tonight. . . ." These simple, clear words, memory-cued by rhythm and rhyme, invite instant playback. The invitation "Now say it with me!" puts the choral-speaking mechanism in motion.

Almost every rhymed and metered poem in the primary grades can be enhanced through choral speaking. In addition, shared speaking encourages participation without risk. Shyness, fear of making mistakes, and the embarrassment of forgetting lines are all overcome as one speaks with the group.

This technique is also an aid to reading, particularly when used in the early years. As students recite together, they may rely partly on memory and partly on print to guide them. In this way, the "difficult" words become familiar in print.

Avoiding the Sing-Song Pitfall. In choral reading, metered poetry may begin to sound "sing-song," a mere exercise in reciting rhythm without the intended interpretation of meaning. One way to avoid this pitfall is *not* to confine intermediate- and upper-grade choral reading to rhymed and metered poetry. An alternative is to let the sing-song pleasure of a metered poem run half its course, and then begin to introduce variety into the reading. Another is to concentrate on the poem's meaning. You might begin by reading a few lines of a poem and asking questions like these: "Who is saying these lines? How should the lines be said? In a puzzled voice? In a sad voice? With a laughing tone? What is happening in the poem? How can we show this feeling with our voices?" Such attention to meaning, even with nonsense poetry, will help direct the rhythm and sound away from a sing-song pattern and toward vocal variety in pace and volume.

Another way to avoid sing-song interpretations is to divide the choral reading so that *all* speakers do not read *all* of the lines. Some lines can be read in unison by all speakers, but some will be read by a subgroup or by one speaker.

PUPPETRY

Puppet shows hold fascination for children and adults. Students who a moment ago complained ''I can't think of what to say'' are suddenly released when ''it is the puppets who do the talking.''

Construction of Puppets. In order to leave time for the production, select one of the following easy-to-make puppets.

1. *Hand puppets*. A simple hand puppet may be no more than an old sock stretched over the hand and adjusted so that the curved palm of the hand opens and closes like a mouth. The face of the hand puppet can be dabbed on with tempera paint or constructed from yarn, buttons, and sewn-on shapes of cloth.
2. *Stick puppets*. A stick puppet may consist of a painted or cut-paper face on a flat surface such as a paper plate stapled or pasted on the end of a tongue depressor.
3. *Fist puppets*. A fist puppet is more elaborate than those mentioned above. The fist puppet's head is modeled out of papier-maché or other lightweight material, such as cotton or crushed paper with heavy paper covering. Features are applied with poster paint. The puppet's eyes should be larger than life to provide emphasis. A cardboard cylinder big enough to fit over the index finger is embedded at the neck of the puppet. The puppet's costume can be cloth that is cut and sewn to be gathered at the puppet's neck, with sleeves that fit over the puppeteer's thumb and fifth finger.

Practice and Performance. Give students time to experiment with their newly constructed puppets—to play with voice and movement. When they are ready to perform, they may present the puppet show as Story Theater, where one or more readers read the story while puppeteers manipulate the puppets to show the action. The puppeteers may also perform the story on their own, using creative dramatics techniques to improvise dialogue and gesture. Finally, scripts may be selected or prepared: some students may read the speeches while other students manipulate the puppets; or the puppeteers may speak the puppets' dialogue as they manipulate them.

READERS THEATRE

In Readers Theatre—the term is usually spelled that way, without an apostrophe—students read orally from scripts that are often based on selections from literature. Play scripts, then, are especially suitable for reading with this technique, since characters' speeches are already indicated. The technique is also adaptable for use with stories and poems that contain considerable direct conversation.

Specialists in the Readers Theatre technique indicate that selections may be abridged or occasionally paraphrased for script purposes. They warn, however, that scripts are to be used only for specific performance; to circulate scripts extensively or to use them for wide public performance is against copyright law.

How It Works. Similar to actors in a play, the performers in Readers Theatre ''take roles''; they speak lines assigned to characters or to one or more narrators. But unlike actors, Readers Theatre performers do not move about a stage; they hold scripts in hand or place them on music stands or desks. A few gestures and changes in position are permitted if these help the interpretation, but the real effect of the literary selection must come from the readers' oral interpretation of characters and narration. Hence the suggestions for interpretive oral reading (page T39) are appropriate for Readers Theatre practice as well.

The prospect of a Readers Theatre performance is highly motivating to students. Once roles are assigned, they do not need to be told to practice their oral reading. They will do so on their own, especially when they can practice with a partner or a "dialogue director" who can give instant feedback on whether or not the character is "coming through" in the reading.

The Importance of the Director.
The presentation can be improved by a good director who tells the readers how an audience might receive their efforts. Who should be the director? A student? The teacher? A parent volunteer? Any one of these will do if he or she can bravely but not threateningly stop the rehearsal at almost any point to offer advice: "I didn't *hear* how angry the two trolls were when Prince Lini refused them. Try that again" (*Half a Kingdom*, Level 4). Of course, the director must find a balance between expecting too much in a performance and permitting flaccid, unthinking reading. Students respond to direction that asks for, but does not demand, a lively, varied interpretation.

Finally, the finished production may be performed for an audience. Performers may sit or stand side by side, facing the audience, or they may position themselves so that two opposing characters face each other, the narrators off to one side and slightly closer to the audience. The audience, the performance area, and the likely arrangement of readers should be decided upon before final rehearsals begin, so that the readers feel they are working toward a well-planned, polished performance.

STORY THEATER

Interpretive oral reading is combined with "acting out" in Story Theater. One or more students read aloud the selection, which should be a story or a poem with plenty of action. Simultaneously, a group of "players" performs the actions described in the reading. In addition, players may sometimes act as scenery. For example, several may portray a wall, a tree, or the window of a house.

How It Works. Story Theater begins with attentive reading and discussion of the story to be presented. Movement, or mime, can be encouraged as a natural extension of inference questions: "Show us how the lizard moves his head from side to side. Show how the hawk soars over the land, looking for the ring" ("The Wedding of the Hawk," Level 6). Roles are assigned or chosen by volunteers. Players develop their parts as they listen to the oral readers' rendition of the story; oral readers practice their skill until they can vary their pace to accommodate the pace of the players. The final performance, then, is a combination of oral reading and mimed action.

After its completion, the performance should be evaluated by the participants, using questions such as the following: *Which segments in the reading gave life to the story? What did the players do to make certain actions vivid? When a player was present but not specifically mentioned in a moment of action, what did he or she do? Did the player* freeze, *standing still so that attention was directed to the action, or did the player* react *to what was happening?*

Would a different response have been more effective?

The critique, or evaluation, may be followed by a second performance, and students may then note improvements.

Choosing Appropriate Selections.

For primary-grade children, Story Theater works well with nursery rhymes and other simple action poems. It seems especially suited to folk tales that highlight action and do not contain a great deal of dialogue. Intermediate- and upper-level students, however, may wish to experiment with Story Theater productions in which players speak lines of dialogue.

CREATIVE DRAMATICS/ IMPROVISATION

A story or a poem is read. During the discussion that follows, the teacher says, *"Show* us what you mean." A student gestures, mimes a series of actions, or speaks a line in a certain way to demonstrate a character or a description. From such a simple, brief beginning can come the activity often called *creative dramatics*. Creative dramatics is especially valuable for developing skills of inference, as students must infer the actions and motives that characters would be likely to display within the framework of the story. The inferring activity shapes and implements both action and motive. It thus goes a step beyond the more passive inference brought forward through discussion.

First Steps.

Creative dramatics develops gradually. Begin by having students identify *one* crucial scene they would like to play. Then have them "try on" characters and develop gestures, facial expressions, and a manner of speech for each. Lines of dialogue may be quoted directly from the story, but memorizing should not get in the way of the playing. Instead, encourage players to *improvise* dialogue in the spirit of the story and scene.

Once the improvisation is under way, there may be a tendency for the scene to go on and on. If this happens, stop the action. (A signal from you, such as the single word "Curtain," can be used to stop the action without embarrassing anyone.) Immediately ask students to evaluate the playing: "What was strong in the playing? What seemed to be going wrong?" At this point, ask the group, players and observers alike, to reread the scene.

Insight into Character.

Geraldine Siks, an expert on creative dramatics procedure, offers a further suggestion: Have each player identify first the *big purpose* of his or her character in terms of the entire story, and then the character's *little purpose* in the scene that is being played. In addition, character traits and emotions should be discussed.[7] During this discussion, the focus should be on the characters, not the players. Say, for example: "The old man must show that he is terrified of the sea monster," not "You should act more terrified when you look at the sea monster."

Following evaluation, the scene should be replayed. Further evaluation should note any improvements in the playing.

The Need for Brief but Frequent Sessions.

The single-scene sessions should be brief, perhaps no longer than ten minutes in primary grades and fifteen minutes in intermediate and upper grades. Frequent sessions, perhaps two per week, are recommended by most experts as the best way to move from creative dramatics to meaningful dramatic interpretation.

---

7. Geraldine Brain Siks, *Drama with Children* (New York: Harper & Row, 1977), p. 119.

From Scene to Story. At all levels, dramatizing a single scene can lead to playing an entire story once the improvisation process runs smoothly. When an entire story is dramatized, pace and structure become more important than ever. The story must progress without having dialogue or action distract from its central focus. Winifred Ward, perhaps the best-known expert in the field of creative dramatics in schools, advises that planners and players must "concentrate on essentials," shortening or omitting scenes that contribute to the written story but do not move the drama forward. Scenes themselves often require "tightening," which involves highlighting the essential movement and dialogue while omitting the nonessential. Ward's basic evaluation question at this point is "Did the scene *move*?"[8] Attention must also be directed to the clear presentation of the story's problems in an early scene and to the build-up through successive scenes to a climax and solution.

Role Playing. An extension of creative dramatics is *role playing*, a technique that requires extrapolation. In role playing, a story is read up to the point at which a problem is encountered but not solved. Students discuss what the main characters will do about the situation. Roles are assigned, possible solutions are enacted, and the results are evaluated by asking, "Is this what the main characters *would* do? Is this what they *should* do?"

One of the values of role playing is evident when students return to the story to read the author's solution to the problem they have resolved. They do so with heightened interest, for they have taken an active role in predicting the story's outcome.

PLAY PRODUCTION

Informal Presentations. In the classroom, a play script may be presented informally without scenery, costumes, or memorization, and with minimal movement. An informal presentation provides practice in characterization and timing. It also improves speaking skills, especially if readers must project their voices to an audience. The informal presentation can be enhanced if it is recorded on tape as a "radio play" with background music and sound effects. The tape may then be played for the readers' enjoyment and evaluation.

Formal Productions. Formal production based on a play script requires much more time and planning, and it deserves an audience. It may also require a budget. Still, the excitement of a formal production of a play often makes the effort worthwhile. So, too, do the other rewards: the literary learning that results from extended close work with the play script, the confidence that arises from successfully portraying characters and incidents, and the poise that comes with performing in a company before an audience.

Preparing Young Students for Play Productions. Students at the primary level need informal experience in drama before attempting a formal play production. Both Story Theater and creative dramatics should come first. Then, when a play script is before the students and the decision is made to present it as a play, they need to become aware of its requirements. Maxine McSweeny[9] reported one group's suggestions for play performance, which were written on the chalkboard by their teacher:

8. Winifred Ward, *Playmaking with Children from Kindergarten Through Junior High School*, 2d ed. (New York: Appleton-Century-Crofts, 1957), p. 138.

9. Maxine McSweeny, *Creative Children's Theatre for Home, School, Church, and Playground* (Cranbury, N.J.: A. S. Barnes, 1974), p. 131.

- Know exactly what to say and do. [They can't make it up in front of an audience.]
- Act so the audience can see what they do.
- Speak so the audience can understand what they say.
- Make the play's story live for the audience.

Suggestions for a Successful Production. Once a class has had some experience with formal play production on a small scale, the following suggestions may help to guide more extensive productions.

1. *Make sure the class has had sufficient experience in oral interpretation and movement before they try to perform a play that requires extensive dialogue and a succession of scenes.*

2. *Make sure the class* likes *the play script.* Talk it over. Ask them to explain the dramatic appeal: "What might an audience like about this play?"

3. *Hold try-outs for all facets of the production, not just for acting roles.* Ask for volunteers to make scenery (drawn, painted, constructed, or hung as a backdrop), to be in charge of props, or to act as dialogue coaches. The actors themselves must be selected carefully, of course. Have them try out by improvisation rather than by reading lines. Ask pairs of students to assume the characters from the play and then to compose speeches and movements to fit a particular scene.

4. *With class participation, make a schedule for rehearsals.* The first session should consist of reading lines, with attention to oral interpretation of character. The second session should begin the *blocking* of action, determining characters' movements about the stage in each scene. In general, movement must be motivated, and a character should not move while another is speaking.

"Stage business"—the use of props and gestures—is included in the blocking of action. At this point actors may carry scripts but they should also devote attention to memorizing lines. Subsequent sessions give practice, scene by scene, in dialogue and action.

5. *When planning scenery, costumes, and lighting, suggest rather than strive for actuality.* Setting may be suggested by scenery sketched on wrapping paper or merely by a backdrop consisting of a curtain or drape. An item of costume, such as a hat or an appropriate jacket, can suffice to designate a character. Lighting need not require footlights or spotlights, but the playing area should be clearly visible to an audience. The playing area itself can be a cleared area in the classroom if a raised stage is not available.

6. *Set aside time for a* dress rehearsal—*a session in which the entire production receives a run-through without interruption.* During this final rehearsal, the director may keep notes so that he or she can comment on the production afterward. The comments should be mainly positive, to encourage the players and crew to do their best. If the performance is to run smoothly, few changes should be made in the production at this point.

7. *Plan to present a formal production before an audience.* Besides offering a means for appreciating the considerable efforts of the cast, crew, and director, the production of a play is intended to provide entertainment for others. Some groups plan more than one performance, for increased experience before an audience.

A Word About Royalties. Some plays, if presented formally, require payment of royalties. Be sure to check the title and copyright pages of a play script for a royalty statement before deciding to put the script into production.

A Sense of Accomplishment. Allot time when the production is over for evaluating what was learned, what was especially satisfying, and what might be done "next time" to make the production process flow more smoothly. Teachers and other adults involved need to remember that play production in schools is for education, appreciation, and pleasure. A good question to consider is this: "Ten years from now will this play be recalled by my students with pleasure and a sense of real accomplishment?"

Let it also be remembered that theater experience with literature is *direct* experience with literature. As author Tove Jansson has a wise character say in *Moomin's Summer Madness*, "A theatre is the most important sort of house in the world, because that's where people are shown what they could be if they wanted, and what they'd like to be if they dared to, and what they really are."[10]

Additional Readings

Provenmire, E. Kingsley. *Choral Speaking and the Verse Choir*. Cranbury, N.J.: A. S. Barnes, 1975. Definitions, procedures, and materials for voice choir are presented, with discussion focused on each age level.

Coger, Lesley Irene, and White, Melvin R. *Readers Theatre Handbook: A Dramatic Approach to Literature*. Rev. ed. Glenview, Ill.: Scott, Foresman, 1973. Definitions, procedures, and "rules" for successful Readers Theatre productions, with helpful case studies of how the procedures have succeeded in schools.

---

10. Tove Jansson, *Moomin's Summer Madness* trans. Ernest Benn, Ltd. (New York: Avon Books, 1955), pp. 105–106.

McCaslin, Nellie. *Creative Drama in the Classroom*, 3d ed. New York: Longman, 1980. This up-to-date edition gives reasons for using pantomime, improvisation, and creative dramatics. It is rich in examples of how to use drama in the classroom, especially for interpretations of poetry and other literary forms.

Visual Arts, Music, and Literature

ART ACTIVITIES

The visual arts offer teachers and students a great variety of activities: drawing and painting, paper cutting, sculpting and modeling, constructing and printmaking. Any one of these can stir the students' imaginations and provide them with a visual means of responding to literature.

The teacher's choice of which art activity will enhance a literary experience can be guided by class discussions of a particular selection. For example, if the discussion focuses on the *setting*, then students might sketch the setting or visualize it through collage. As they reread a description of a setting in a story or a poem, urge the students to develop a mental image. Then using pencil, crayon, pastel, charcoal, or another sketching instrument, they can sketch quickly on paper the scene in their imaginations. Later, details may be added and the scene may be finished with tempera paint, water color, chalk, or another medium.

Characters in literature also may fire the imagination. Following a discussion of a main character's traits, invite students to model that character from clay. Encourage them *not* to try to represent how the character looked, but rather what the character was like and the impression that character made upon the readers. Finished clay figures, dried or baked in a kiln, can be displayed against a painted or constructed background of the story's setting. Students in the upper grades might sculpt figures from plaster of paris blocks.

In addition to individual art projects, you may sometimes wish to encourage group projects in response to literature. For example, students could create a mural or a large map of a "journey" story, labeling each place and major event in the story. Students also could make an *accordion book* by the following method: the class identifies the main events in the story; each student sketches one of the events; the sketches are arranged in order and then connected by loose stitching or metal rings. The result is a visual display of the story sequence.

MUSIC ACTIVITIES

The rhythms and sounds of words have their counterparts in the rhythms and sounds of music. Poems with strong rhythms or pleasant-sounding lines can inspire song making. To create songs from poems, have students read a poem several times to bring out the rhythm, phrasing, and mood. Use choral speaking techniques to do this. Then have students experiment with beat and sample melodies, progressing line-by-line through the poem. When the final song version is put together, tape the melody or quickly notate it above a written version of the poem.

Musical instruments can be used to create sounds that will heighten the mood for oral reading or any performance of literature. A "signature tune," for instance, may announce the entrance of each character in the telling of a folk tale. Such tunes can be composed on a homemade xylophone, recorder, or kalimba. To stress the rhythm in a poem, use rhythm sticks, various types of drums, sand blocks, and maracas. Musical instruments may also be used to help establish the setting of a story or a play.

Listening to music may also enhance literary appreciation. To seek a literal tie between a literary selection and a musical selection is unnecessary. For example, no composer has written a symphony, ballet, or specific program music to accompany the Norwegian folk tale "The Three Billy Goats Gruff" (Level 1, Reader), yet children can find the troll and the setting of the drama in numerous works of the Norwegian composer Edvard Greig. Played before, during, and after the reading of a selection, such music adds impact while developing the students' listening abilities.

These are only a few of the boundless opportunities to promote literary appreciation and response through the visual arts and music. Boundless, too, is the pleasure to be gained.

Additional Readings

Gaitskell, Charles D., and Hurwitz, Al. *Children and Their Art*. 3d ed. New York: Harcourt Brace Jovanovich, 1975. This book presents a synthesis of child development and art development. It includes many examples that help explain how to encourage child development with art education.

Taylor, Gail Cohen. "Music in Language Arts Instruction." *Language Arts* 58, no. 3 (March 1981): 363–367. This review of recent writing on the topic includes a section on music as an aid to story enjoyment and comprehension as well as a list of resources for teachers.

Poetry and the Teacher

Myra Cohn Livingston

I am myself,
of all my atom parts I am the sum.
And out of my blood and my brain
I make my own interior weather,
my own sun and rain.
Imprint my mark upon the world,
whatever I shall become.

Eve Merriam, "Thumbprint"

ROBERT FROST has written that a poem "begins in delight and ends in wisdom." The Irish poet James Stephens tells us that "What the heart knows today the head will understand tomorrow." In these words both poets suggest one of the most meaningful ways of introducing children to poetry: to infect with *delight,* stress the *joy,* approach through the *heart,* and know that wisdom and understanding will follow. It makes all the difference.

Children grow into poetry, beginning with Mother Goose. From the first time they hear rhyming verses that tell a small story, that play with words, that move along with bouncing rhythms, that stress rhyme, they are affirming a basic need to listen with both heart and movement—to respond with pleasure.

Jack be nimble,
Jack be quick,
Jack jump over
The candlestick.

Even nonsense poems allow them to test their own knowledge of what is true and what is not, to improve their self-images, and to be able to laugh both at others and at themselves:

Far and few, far and few,
Are the lands where the Jumblies live:
Their heads are green, and their hands
are blue;
And they went to sea in a sieve.

Edward Lear, "The Jumblies"

New discoveries, thoughts, dreams, widely ranging emotions surround children as they grow up. Poetry mirrors their experiences through a more sophisticated handling of imagery, rhythm, and sound. What distinguishes poetry from other forms of literature is a rhythm that almost invites our bodies to move, our fingers to tap, our feet to dance; combinations of words that make us wish to repeat them aloud; rhymes, oftentimes, that encourage us to make up our own series of sounds; and a sort of irresistible music that engages heart, mind, and body. From the simplest folk rhyme to the ballad, from the traditional to the most experimental contemporary poem, poetry gives children room where their emotions and imaginations may run free.

DISCOVERING POETRY

The delight of poetry is in discovery: a new image, a different way of looking, the pleasure of words and rhythms used well, a humorous idea, an eccentric person, a striking metaphor. The delight is in the freedom to choose from among so many kinds of poems the ones that speak to us. The delight is in becoming familiar with riddles and limericks, haiku and counting rhymes, ballads and shape poems. The delight remains so long as children are able to come to a poem and find something of themselves and their world mirrored, extended, or even stretched. The delight allows them to act out the stories in pantomime or dance, to sculpt, to illustrate, to chant the words aloud, alone or with others, to try writing poems of their own, to respond in individual ways to the poetry they hear and read.

In the ten books of the ODYSSEY series, teachers will find verse and poetry to bring delight and pleasure. Here are traditional verses that have long been favorites of young readers, juxtaposed with verse by contemporary poets who write for today's young people. A mixture of light and serious verse spanning centuries and cultures has been selected within the thematic strands to afford a wide choice for both teacher and student. It may certainly happen that some of the selections will not appeal to every child or teacher. All of us hear a different tune. Some enjoy rhyming verse and ordered meter, while others prefer a freer, more open approach to poetry. Humorous verse, limericks, and riddles appeal to some; poetry with a more serious tone, a different mood, to others. Fortunately there are enough poems for all. Both teachers and students should always feel free to pick and choose what is meaningful to them as individuals.

It is here, I believe, that the wisdom and understanding of which Robert Frost and James Stephens spoke become important. Wisdom is *not* the message given by a poem to a reader; wisdom is *not* didacticism cajoling, exhorting, or instructing the reader of a poem to behave in a certain fashion; wisdom is *not* high-flown sentiments in lofty diction. Nor is wisdom achieved by tearing apart a poem to find what figures of speech, what symbolism it may contain. Rather, wisdom is acquired by knowing that as we read poetry we grow in understanding. Wisdom is found by relating our thoughts and emotions as individuals to ourselves and to others about us, to other cultures, other centuries, other places. Wisdom comes in knowing that the best poetry has something to say for each of us if we first make the commitment to find the delight. Wisdom also implies that *com*prehending is not nearly so important as *ap*prehending. As John Ciardi has pointed out, it is important that we never ask "*What* does a poem mean?" but rather "*How* does a poem mean?" For Ciardi, the skillful combination of idea, form, words, and rhythm separates real poetry from mere pleasantries put into verse form.

Most likely we will not want to speak to children about methods of delighting or wisdom and understanding. What we can do is try to show them that poetry is part of life. Poetry has something to say about the way we view ourselves, our world, and everything in that world from a drop of rain to mirrors in the Fun House to our feelings about ourselves. Poetry can be funny, it can be sad. It is not, as many believe, a unit of study we get once a year filled with iambic pentameter and some poems to memorize.

Because of the increasing number of fine poetry anthologies available, it is possible for teachers in all grades to relate poetry to almost any subject. History might be studied using some of the folk poetry of America. Numerous poems deal with science and math. The ODYSSEY Teacher's Editions offer a wide variety of suggestions for integrating poetry with other arts— painting, dancing, creative writing, and dramatics, to name just a few.

Our most difficult job as teachers today may well lie in the need to elicit imaginative responses. In a world that promotes an unusual amount of passivity, reliance on mass media, and a great deal of programmed response, teachers need to touch the imagination of each child, to encourage this individual reaction to what is heard or read. In a single classroom there may be but a handful of children who respond to a given poem, but this reaction should be praised and nurtured. What happens when a poem and the right listener, the right reader, come together can be magic.

SHARING POETRY IN THE CLASSROOM

It will come as no surprise to teachers that few children today hear nursery rhymes at home. The classroom may well be the first place children hear poetry, and the teacher may well be the first person who reads poetry to them aloud. No matter what age or level of the students, poetry should be read aloud as often as possible.

Many of the poems in the ten ODYSSEY readers are suitable for individual and choral reading. Students can organize group readings of poems or memorize them for the joy of it. Many balk at the idea of memorization, but if a student especially likes a poem, the results can be wonderful! Whole classes have put on poetry programs to entertain other classes until the entire school becomes infected with the joy of performing. Again, if imagination is encouraged by the teacher, the students benefit not only from their personal response to poetry but grow with their hearts and minds to bring its enjoyment to others. Here are a few suggestions to help you get started.

1. *Choose poems you like and those you think your class will like.* Teachers cannot elicit enthusiasm for work they themselves do not enjoy. Be aware that riddles, limericks, and light verse will always be received well, but that other kinds of poetry will help young people grow in their perceptions and relationships with others.

2. *Encourage students to find verses and poems and share them with the class.*

3. *Experiment with different ways of reading the sounds and rhythms of poems.* One way to read a poem is to read each line as a separate idea followed by a pause.

Who has seen the wind? (pause)
Neither you nor I: (pause)
But when the trees bow down their
    heads (pause)
The wind is passing by.

> Christina Rossetti,
> "Who Has Seen the Wind?"

Another way is to pause at the punctuation in a line. In this stanza, then, the question mark at the end of line 1 indicates a pause, as does the colon at the end of line 2. In the third line, however, one could either pause after the word *heads* or read the last two lines as one long sentence. There is no right or wrong.

4. *Don't be afraid to make mistakes when you read poems aloud.* Everyone does. If you flub a reading, pick up and start again—this will help minimize the students' embarrassment when they make mistakes in their own readings. Both teacher and students can learn together.

5. *Read with your heart rather than your head.* If you wish to laugh as you read, do so. When a poem is sad, don't hide your sadness; let it enter your voice just as you would let happiness.

Children know what emotions are—do not underestimate their ability to know if you are reading with honesty. They would much rather have a flawed, sincere reading from you than the perfectly enunciated recitation on a tape or record.

Don't be afraid to make the leap. Leave your head in arithmetic, in history, in social studies, in science; and bring your heart and sense of delight to poetry! You may astound yourself; you will astound your students—and together you will begin a love for poetry that you may never before have imagined possible.

Myra Cohn Livingston, ODYSSEY's poetry consultant, is Poet-in-Residence for the Beverly Hills Unified School District and a Senior Instructor at UCLA Extension. The author of thirty books, she has received many awards for her poetry, including the National Council of Teachers of English Award for Excellence in Poetry for Children, which was awarded her in 1980.

Bibliography

Books About Poetry

Ciardi, John. *How Does a Poem Mean?* Boston: Houghton Mifflin, 1959.

Hughes, Ted. *Poetry Is.* New York: Doubleday, 1970.

Kennedy, X. J. *An Introduction to Poetry.* 4th ed. Boston: Little, Brown, 1978.

Individual Poets

Bodecker, N. M. *Hurry, Hurry, Mary Dear! and Other Nonsense Poems.* New York: Atheneum, 1976.

Brooks, Gwendolyn. *Bronzeville Boys and Girls.* New York: Harper & Bros., 1956.

Clifton, Lucille. *Everett Anderson's Year.* New York: Holt, Rinehart & Winston, 1974.

Farber, Norma. *Small Wonders.* New York: Coward, McCann & Geoghegan, 1979.

Fisher, Aileen. *Out in the Dark and Daylight.* New York: Harper & Row, 1980.

Holman, Felice. *I Hear You Smiling and Other Poems.* New York: Charles Scribner's Sons, 1973.

Kuskin, Karla. *Dogs & Dragons, Trees & Dreams.* New York: Harper & Row, 1980.

McCord, David. *One at a Time.* Boston: Little, Brown, 1978.

Milne, A. A. *When We Were Very Young.* New York: E. P. Dutton, 1924.

Smith, William Jay. *Laughing Time: Nonsense Poems.* New York: Delacorte Press, 1980.

Thurman, Judith. *Flashlight and Other Poems.* New York: Atheneum, 1976.

Watson, Clyde. *Father Fox's Pennyrhymes.* New York: Thomas Y. Crowell, 1971.

Anthologies

Adoff, Arnold, ed. *My Black Me: A Beginning Book on Black Poetry.* New York: E. P. Dutton, 1974.

Behn, Harry, trans. *Cricket Songs.* New York: Harcourt Brace Jovanovich, 1964. Haiku attuned to young people.

Brewton, John E., and Blackburn, Lorraine A., comps. *They've Discovered a Head in the Box for the Bread and Other Laughable Limericks.* New York: Harper & Row, 1978.

Cole, William, ed. *The Birds and the Beasts Were There.* Cleveland: World, 1963. Poems about animals for every reader.

De la Mare, Walter, ed. *Come Hither.* New York: Alfred A. Knopf, 1957. A favorite collection of traditional poetry.

Houston, James, ed. *Songs of the Dream People: Chants and Images from the Indians and Eskimos of North America.* New York: Atheneum, 1972.

Wood, Ray, ed. *Fun in American Folk Rhymes.* Philadelphia: J. B. Lippincott, 1952.

Wordless Picture Books and the Teacher *Rosemary Salesi*

Once upon a time there lived a little boy and a dog. They wanted to catch a frog for a friend and pet. They started down the hill and a branch was in there [their] way so the boy cut it down and put it in front of him. Then he started off again and right before him was a frog. He ran towards it and triped [tripped] over the branch and fell right into the water with dog and all. . . .

Sarah Shubert, First Grade

SARAH SHUBERT'S STORY, her own retelling of Mercer Mayer's book *A Boy, a Dog, and a Frog*[1] (in ODYSSEY Primer, Level 1), is just one example of how students can respond to a *wordless picture book*, a book in which pictures explain a concept or tell a story. Using invented spellings for some words, Sarah wrote her story after several short classroom activities: looking at the book; predicting what happened next in the story; and telling the story in sequence with the rest of the class. This lesson was in late March; for the previous three months, Sarah and her classmates kept diaries and wrote a short response paper each day. The few stories the first graders wrote, however, usually lacked a developed middle and an adequate ending; only a few were complete narratives. With the support of the plot, sequence, and characterization provided by Mercer Mayer's illustrations, well over half of the children wrote complete stories. Some, like Sarah, even observed the conventions of traditional storytelling, beginning with "Once upon a time" and ending with "And they lived happily ever after."

WHAT ARE WORDLESS PICTURE BOOKS?

For some teachers, the existence of wordless books and their use in the classroom may seem to be recent developments; but the first contemporary wordless picture books, such as Ruth Carroll's *What Whiskers Did*,[2] appeared in the early 1930s. In the 1960s and 1970s, many illustrators rediscovered this unique format and explored it further. They found that by using a series of sequenced illustrations with few or no words, they could introduce, develop, and eventually resolve a story problem. At this writing, over seventy-five illustrators have contributed wordless picture books to the growing body of children's literature, and each year brings more.

What is surprising about these books is their considerable variation in content, format, and style of art. There are two predominant types: *concept books*, which primarily deal with the alphabet, shapes, numbers, and such nonfiction subjects as

1. Mercer Mayer, *A Boy, a Dog, and a Frog* (New York: Dial Press, 1967).

2. Ruth Carroll, *What Whiskers Did* (New York: Henry Z. Walck, 1965).

the Apollo mission or a life cycle in nature; and *wordless stories*, which use sequenced pictures to move from an introduction of characters and problems to a climax and conclusion.[3] In a wordless story, the characters' facial expressions and actions aid the reader in deciphering the plot.

Teachers find wordless books to be an imaginative resource for promoting oral language development, storytelling, and writing skills at all grade levels. Students enjoy and think through the stories at the same time, and eventually most want to share the fun by retelling them to others.[4] Because the books call forth the children's own language, they provide opportunities for exploring concepts and creating stories.[5] The stories the children write can be used as reading material for the entire class. But perhaps most importantly, the use of wordless books can foster a positive attitude toward all books and reading.

Exposure to wordless books will benefit students now and in the future. In our visually oriented society, the ability to see the visual whole and the significance of each detail, as well as the ability to express oneself fluently, are needed by everyone.

THE TEACHER'S ROLE: GENERAL CONSIDERATIONS

Reading a wordless picture book should be an enjoyable experience for students. The student's language abilities and prior experiences, as well as the books themselves, will help determine success. In sharing these books, it is necessary to observe whether the children enjoy them. If the motivation of enjoyment is not there, avoid follow-up activities.

Except when used for lessons in making predictions, the entire book should be "read" initially without interruption. Since comprehension depends on how well the students perceive minor details and subtleties in a story, a second or third viewing, coupled with exploratory activities, will help students appreciate and respond to it more fully. Filmstrips of wordless picture books, such as those produced by Weston Woods Studios, Inc., enable large groups of students to enjoy the same story simultaneously and allow the teacher to focus attention on selected elements.

Beginning in the lower grades, wordless books can be used for step-by-step practice in describing characters and actions with words or phrases, then with one complete sentence, two or more sentences, and finally, with a number of sentences in logical order. Since many of the more sophisticated books can be read at either the literal or symbolic level, they work well in heterogeneous groups of students. For example, the problems that bilingual students have with books are lessened because they can label objects, describe actions, or write stories using their own languages. The books are so highly entertaining that the students may be more comfortable using their new language as they share ideas with each other.

---

3. Rosemary A. Salesi, "Reading, That's Easy. It's the Words That Are Tough," *Maine Reading Association Bulletin* (Spring 1973): 3–6.

4. Rosemary A. Salesi, "Books Without Words," *New England Reading Association Journal,* 9 (1973–74): 28–30.

5. Patricia J. Ciancolo, "Using Wordless Books to Teach Reading and Visual Literacy and to Study Literature," *Top of the News,* 29 (April 1973): 226–234.

SPECIFIC TEACHING SUGGESTIONS

The following are some ways to introduce students to wordless picture books. They may also help students gain independence for reading the books on their own.

1. *Suggest that students use the title to guess what might happen in the story.* This will help to prepare them for the events of the story.

2. *When using a wordless picture book that tells a story, be sure the students understand that the book does tell a story.* This is particularly important with preschool and early primary students.

3. *If the students are to work independently, encourage them to examine the entire book first, including the cover, endpapers, title page, and dedication page.* In some books, such as Peter Spier's *Noah's Ark*[6] and Diane De Groat's *Alligator's Toothache,*[7] the stories begin prior to the first page. Inferences are easier to draw when the student has examined the entire story.

4. *Encourage the students to look at illustrations closely and to note details.* Details in the illustrations foreshadow new events, changes in the action, or a subplot.

5. *Ask questions that students should ask themselves when they read alone:* What is happening? Why is it happening? What will happen next? Did I predict correctly? How do I know? What might the characters be saying to each other? What words would describe their actions and feelings?

6. *Have the students examine their wordless picture books several times and talk about them with classmates. Then ask them to close the books and tell the story.* If they use the book in storytelling, both children and adults tend to describe only the details in the pictures, completely ignoring the gaps that occur between them. Storytelling becomes more natural when the book is put aside because the storyteller is more apt to fill in the missing details and feel freer to improvise. The book's content thus provides a structure around which the storyteller can fashion his or her own stories. Creative responses should be praised.

Rosemary Salesi is a widely published author of professional articles and a reading workshop leader. She is currently an associate professor of education at the University of Maine at Orono, where she teaches courses in children's literature and elementary education. She was a classroom teacher for eight years.

Wordless Books for Primary Grades

Although the following selections are intended for primary grades, they need not be limited to a specific age or grade level. In most cases, students enjoy a wider range of wordless books as they mature. Children in preschool and early primary grades generally prefer realistic stories. Older, middle-school students enjoy these as well as the more sophisticated and fanciful books.

Anno, Mitsumasa. *Anno's Counting Book.* New York: Thomas Y. Crowell, 1977.

Briggs, Raymond. *The Snowman.* New York: Random House, 1978.

Carle, Eric. *Do You Want to Be My Friend?* New York: Thomas Y. Crowell, 1971.

Hoban, Tana. *Dig, Drill, Dump, Fill.* New York: Greenwillow Books, 1975.

Krahn, Fernando. *Sebastian and the Mushroom.* New York: Delacorte Press, 1976.

Sugita, Yutaka. *My Friend Little John and Me.* New York: McGraw-Hill, 1973.

Ueno, Noriko. *Elephant Buttons.* New York: Harper & Row, 1973.

---

6. Peter Spier, *Noah's Ark* (Garden City, N.Y.: Doubleday, 1977).

7. Diane De Groat, *Alligator's Toothache* (New York: Crown, 1977).

Resource Center

About the Authors and Illustrators

These notes present some information about the authors and illustrators in this book upon whom material was available. You may wish to read them aloud as you introduce the selections.

Clifton, Lucille   See page 119 of the pupil's textbook for the feature about this poet.

Curtright, Wesley   Born in Georgia in 1910, Wesley Curtright attended schools in various northern and southern states and worked as a clerk for the state of New York. "Heart of the Woods" is from the collection *Golden Slippers;* more of his poems can be found in *The Poetry of the Negro: 1746–1970* and *Negro Voices.*

de la Mare, Walter   Walter de la Mare (1873–1956) is one of the few major poets who wrote for children as well as adults. A writer of rare gifts, de la Mare enjoyed writing poems about witches, ogres, dwarfs, sleep, dreamland, and moonlight. Born in Kent, England, the sixth child of a bank official, he published his first poetry volume, *Songs of Childhood,* in 1902, while a clerk for an oil company. He completed over three hundred poems, twenty stories, sixty retellings of traditional stories for children, and several excellent anthologies.

de Regniers, Beatrice Schenk
Beatrice Schenk de Regniers's books range from her poetic stories to riddle rhymes to picture-book folk tales. "Most of them begin in a meadow," she has said. "I take my notebook and my pencil and go away, alone, to a place where I can be physically in touch with nature."

Galarza, Ernesto   See page 171 of the pupil's textbook for the feature about this poet.

Galdone, Paul   Hungarian-born Paul Galdone has illustrated many award-winning books for young children. "Children's books provide me with much freedom because of their naturally whimsical nature. I particularly enjoy adapting and making picture books of favorite old tales."

Ginsburg, Mirra   Mirra Ginsburg is a well-known editor and translator of Russian and Yiddish folk tales, books, and riddles. She became interested in folk tales as a child: "My childhood home in Russia was almost literally the folk tale world: pinewoods and birches, wide fields and meadows rich with wild flowers closely surrounded our small town. . . ."

Gordon, Shirley   Shirley Gordon writes television scripts and magazine articles, as well as children's books. She also teaches creative writing and children's literature.

Greenfield, Eloise   In 1975 Eloise Greenfield received a citation from the Council on Interracial Books for Children in recognition of her outstanding contributions to children's literature. Whether writing biography, poetry, or fiction, she says, "I want to give children words to love, to grow on."

Holman, Felice Felice Holman began to write during her childhood in New York City. "One of the ways to have people listen to you is to write," she explains. Many of her books are about mysterious or fanciful happenings in the everyday world, and all of them reflect her humor, sense of poetry, and attention to detail.

Isadora, Rachel Rachel Isadora was a ballet dancer in New York City before a foot injury forced her to give up dancing. She now enjoys a new career as a writer and illustrator. In "Max," she was able to combine her love of ballet with her talent for writing.

Jacobs, Joseph Joseph Jacobs (1854–1916) was a leading folklorist, who collected English, Celtic, and Indian fairy tales. He intended, he once said, "to write as a good old nurse will speak when she tells Fairy Tales."

Keith, Eros Eros Keith was not yet in kindergarten when he began drawing pictures to illustrate the stories his grandmother and his father told him. Eros Keith had a difficult time in school, but he slowly became interested in learning. After graduating from art school, he went to New York, where a book editor helped him begin to write and illustrate children's books.

Krahn, Fernando Fernando Krahn, author of more than sixteen books for children and adults, tells all his stories through drawings. A native of Chile who has been drawing since childhood, he began his career in New York as a children's book illustrator and cartoonist for magazines.

Langstaff, John John Langstaff believes that "above all, music should be fun," so it is not surprising that this distinguished concert singer should want to bring music to children. He has taught music, made numerous recordings and performed in concerts for children, and has produced children's television programs about music.

Livingston, Myra Cohn Choose any of Myra Cohn Livingston's poems and you will find her sense of wonder about familiar things—whispers, bike riding, weather, or friends. As she has said, "What more can one offer to the very young . . . than a touchstone to deal with the early daily experiences of feelings, sights, and sounds around them." In 1980 Myra Cohn Livingston received the National Council of Teachers of English Award for Excellence in Poetry for Children.

Lobel, Arnold Arnold Lobel writes about amazing people and curious creatures. "I do my writing in the late afternoon," he has said. "That is a good, quiet time to think about frogs and toads and mice and crickets. . . . Sometimes the stories seem to pour out easily." To date, Lobel has written almost twenty books and illustrated more than forty.

Marshall, James A native of San Antonio, Texas, James Marshall lives in Massachusetts where he attended college and taught French and Spanish in a high school. He has illustrated a number of children's books besides his own writings.

Merriam, Eve For Eve Merriam, "a poem can do just about anything . . . you want it to. It can be solemn or bouncy, gay or sad—as you yourself change your own moods. A poem, in fact, is very much like you. . . ." Eve Merriam is well known for her books *Catch a Little Rhyme, It Doesn't Have to Rhyme,* and *There Is No Rhyme for Silver.* In 1981 she won the National Council of Teachers of English Award for Excellence in Poetry for Children.

Minarik, Else Holmelund See page 76 of the pupil's textbook for the feature about this author.

Mizumura, Kazue /kä·zoō·ä′ mē·zoō′·mû·rä/ Kazue Mizumura began to teach painting and to work as a commercial artist in Japan after she lost her husband and child in the Second World War. In 1955 she came to the United States to attend art school. Later, while working as a textile designer, she began to illustrate books for children and adults. Writing her own books—most of them on themes in nature—gave her a chance to explore her talent further.

Moore, Lilian As a book editor and the author of over twenty books for children, Lilian Moore "never understood why people thought that easy-to-read material for children had to be clunky and dull." Her own poems are anything but dull, whether she is writing about strange, scary happenings or about butterflies.

Parish, Peggy Peggy Parish was born in South Carolina and has taught school in a coal-mining region of Kentucky, in Oklahoma, and in New York City. Her writing career began with stories she wrote for her pupils.

Reynolds, Malvina Malvina Reynolds composed songs reflecting modern-day life and her personal values. "You Can't Make a Turtle Come Out" is from her record *Artichokes, Griddle Cakes, and Other Good Things.*

Sendak, Maurice See page 32 of the pupil's textbook for the feature about this author-illustrator.

Snyder, Zilpha Keatley Zilpha Keatley Snyder grew up in California during the Depression and World War II. Like many others at that time, her family had difficulty making ends meet. "My world might have been quite narrow and uninteresting if it had not been for two magical ingredients— animals and books. . . ." Still a believer in "fairy godmothers, some kinds of ghosts, and all kinds of magical omens," she now writes fantasies about magic in real life.

Udry, Janice May Janice May Udry was a teacher in a Chicago nursery school when she wrote her first book, *A Tree Is Nice.* She has written many others, including several Mary Jo books, which portray a young girl in true-to-life situations. Udry has said, "All my books come from remembering my own childhood and from . . . watching my daughters grow up."

White, Anne Terry Anne Terry White has been a teacher, a social worker, and an editor, as well as a writer. She speaks Russian and French, and loves to travel. Though most of her writings are on historical subjects, she also has adapted many classic stories and books for children, including *Aesop's Fables.*

Poetry for Reading Aloud

The following poems are recommended as related reading in the annotated lessons for this level.

SOLOMON GRUNDY
A Mother Goose rhyme

Solomon Grundy,
Born on a Monday,
Christened on Tuesday,
Married on Wednesday,
Took ill on Thursday,
Worse on Friday,
Died on Saturday,
Buried on Sunday.
This is the end
Of Solomon Grundy.

TEENY TINY GHOST
A poem by Lilian Moore

A teeny, tiny ghost
no bigger than a mouse,
at most,
lived in a great big house.

It's hard to haunt
a great big house
when you're a teeny tiny ghost
no bigger than a mouse,
at most.

He did what he could do.

So every dark and stormy night—
the kind that shakes a house with fright—
if you stood still and listened right,
you'd hear a
teeny
tiny

BOO!

From
GRANDFATHER
A poem by Shirley Crawford

Grandfather dies, I weep.
Grandfather buried, I am left alone.
When I am dead, who will cry?
When I am buried, who will be alone?

Music for Songs in Level 2

OH, A-HUNTING WE WILL GO
From an old song with new verses by John Langstaff and friends

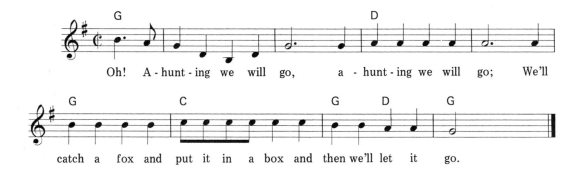

Oh! A-hunt-ing we will go, a - hunt-ing we will go; We'll

catch a fox and put it in a box and then we'll let it go.

Oh, a-hunting we will go, A-hunting we will go; We'll catch a goat And put it in a boat, And then we'll let it go!	Oh, a-hunting we will go, A-hunting we will go; We'll catch a skunk And put it in a bunk, And then we'll let it go!	Oh, a-hunting we will go, A-hunting we will go; We'll catch a brontosaurus And put it in a chorus, And then we'll let it go!

YOU CAN'T MAKE A TURTLE COME OUT
Words and music by Malvina Reynolds

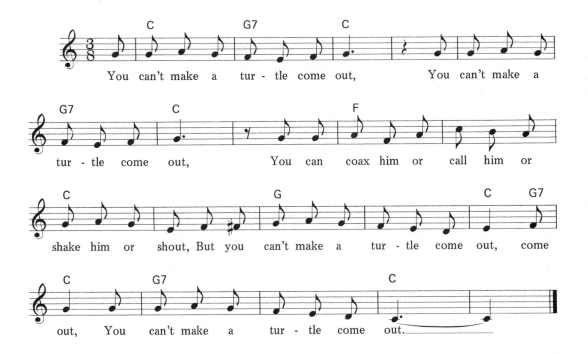

If he wants to stay in his shell,
If he wants to stay in his shell,
You can knock on the door but you can't
   ring the bell,
And you can't make a turtle come out,
   come out,
You can't make a turtle come out.

Be kind to your four-footed friends,
Be kind to your four-footed friends,
A poke makes a turtle retreat at both ends,
And you can't make a turtle come out,
   come out,
You can't make a turtle come out.

So you'll have to patiently wait,
So you'll have to patiently wait,
And when he gets ready, he'll open the
   gate,
But you can't make a turtle come out,
   come out,
You can't make a turtle come out.

And when you forget that he's there,
And when you forget that he's there,
He'll be walking around with his head in the
   air,
But you can't make a turtle come out,
   come out,
You can't make a turtle come out.

Professional Resources for the Teacher

Baskin, Barbara H., and Harris, Karen H. *Books for the Gifted Child.* New York: R. R. Bowker, 1980. An annotated list of almost 150 books for gifted children from kindergarten to upper grades, accompanied by several chapters on the historical and social problems of the gifted child.

Cianciolo, Patricia Jean, ed. *Picture Books for Children.* Chicago: American Library Association, 1973. This list of picture books is annotated with story synopses and art critiques. Categories of interest include Me and My Family, Other People, The World I Live In, and The Imaginative World.

Cullinan, Bernice E., et al. *Literature and the Child.* New York: Harcourt Brace Jovanovich, 1981. Along with selections of outstanding books, this book discusses criteria in choosing books for children and presents many practical teaching ideas.

Huck, Charlotte S. *Children's Literature in the Elementary School.* 3d rev. ed. New York: Holt, Rinehart & Winston, 1979. A reliable, comprehensive aid for understanding children's literature, for becoming familiar with classic and contemporary books, and for using books in the classroom.

Larrick, Nancy. *A Parent's Guide to Children's Reading.* 4th rev. ed. New York: Doubleday, 1975. An annotated listing of recommended books.

Livingston, Myra Cohn. *When You Are Alone/It Keeps You Capone: An Approach to Creative Writing with Children.* New York: Atheneum, 1973.

Lukens, Rebecca J. *A Critical Handbook of Children's Literature.* Glenview, Ill.:

Scott, Foresman, 1976. Discusses the elements used to evaluate all literature—character, plot, setting, theme, point of view, style, and tone—and relates them to examples from children's books.

Moffett, James, and Wagner, Betty J. *Student Centered Language Arts and Reading, K–13: A Handbook for Teachers.* 2nd ed. Boston: Houghton Mifflin, 1976.

Recommended Reading for the Student

Most of the books recommended in this bibliography are available in hardcover. Some materials, however, are listed as paperbacks because they were originally published in that form or because a hardcover version was not available for review. All of the books are divided into the categories of **easy, average,** and **challenging,** which indicate the reading levels of these books. The category **read aloud** indicates books that a teacher might read to the students.

Easy

Alexander, Martha. *Bobo's Dream.* New York: Dial Press, 1970. A wordless picture book. A small dog named Bobo dreams about his chance to protect his young master.

Allen, Jeffrey. *Mary Alice Operator Number 9.* Boston: Little, Brown & Co., 1975. Telephone operator Mary Alice is a friendly duck who gives the time over the telephone. When she gets sick, Boss Chicken must choose a replacement from the eager animals who apply for her job.

Briggs, Raymond. *The Snowman.* New York: Random House, 1978. A wordless picture story about the adventures of a small boy and a snowman who comes to life.

Lobel, Arnold. *On Market Street.* New York: Greenwillow Books, 1981. The simple text describes all the things a shopper sees during a walk along Market Street. Intriguing, detailed illustrations hold interest through several readings.

Rice, Eve. *Once in a Wood: Ten Tales from Aesop.* New York: Greenwillow Books, 1979. Simply-told tales with rhyming morals.

Average

Aliki. *Digging Up Dinosaurs.* New York: Thomas Y. Crowell, 1981. This book surveys the procedures scientists use in finding and preserving fossils.

Blaine, Marge. *The Terrible Thing that Happened at Our House.* New York: Four Winds Press, 1975. As her mother returns to work, a young girl tries to cope in a household turned upside down.

Gackenback, Dick. *Hound and Bear.* New York: Houghton Mifflin, Seabury Press, 1976. Hound enjoys playing tricks on his friend Bear. A story with three episodes.

Galdone, Paul. *The Three Billy Goats Gruff.* New York: Houghton Mifflin, Seabury Press, 1973.

Ginsburg, Mirra. *How the Sun Was Brought Back to the Sky.* New York: Macmillan, 1975. When the sun doesn't shine for three days, five determined chicks leave their mother and set out to find it.

Gordon, Shirley. *Crystal Is My Friend.* New York: Harper & Row, 1978. Susan invites Crystal to sleep over and must let Crystal, as the guest, have her way.

———. *Happy Birthday, Crystal.* New York: Harper & Row, 1981. When Susan arrives at Crystal's for a "private" birthday party, she meets Sherri, who also wants to be Crystal's friend.

Isadora, Rachel. *Ben's Trumpet.* New York: Greenwillow Books, 1979. A Caldecott Honor book that tells about a young boy's dream to learn to play the trumpet.

———. *"No, Agatha!"* New York: Greenwillow Books, 1980. An independent Agatha seems to be a rebellious tomboy as she prowls a luxury liner during a cruise in the late 1800s.

———. *Jesse & Abe.* New York: Greenwillow Books, 1981. With the backstage of a theater as a setting, a simple tale of the love and concern of Jesse for his grandfather becomes exciting, tense, and dramatic.

Keller, Beverly. *Fiona's Flea.* New York: Coward, McCann & Geoghegan, 1981. Though Fiona objects to cruel treatment of animals, she helps plan for a flea show because she knows the fleas will be well treated. Another book about Fiona is *Fiona's Bee.*

MacLachlan, Patricia. *Through Grandpa's Eyes.* New York: Harper & Row, 1980. Young John comes to know his grandfather's house as his grandfather does—through all his senses except sight.

Parish, Peggy. *Dinosaur Time.* New York: Harper & Row, 1974. The author names and describes several dinosaurs. An excerpt from *Dinosaur Time* can be found on page 174.

Rockwell, Anne and Rockwell, Harlow. *Olly's Pollywogs.* New York: Doubleday & Co., 1970. A close-up view of the birth and growth of frogs.

Udry, Janice May. *What Mary Jo Shared.* Chicago: Albert Whitman, 1966. Mary Jo wants to share something special with her class, but she has difficulty finding the right thing.

———. *What Mary Jo Wanted.* Chicago: Albert Whitman, 1968. Though Mary Jo gets the dog she always wanted, she faces the problem of keeping her lonely puppy from whining all night.

Challenging

Aardema, Verna. *Why Mosquitos Buzz in People's Ears.* New York: Dial Press, 1975. In this African pourquoi tale, a pesky mosquito causes a series of problems and has all the jungle animals in an uproar.

Brothers Grimm. *About Wise Men & Simpletons: Twelve Tales from Grimm.* New York: Macmillan, 1971. Includes the tale "The Elves and the Shoemaker."

Froman, Robert. *Seeing Things.* New York: Thomas Y. Crowell, 1974. A collection of Froman's concrete poetry.

Werth, Kurt. *Molly and the Giant.* New York: Parents' Magazine Press, 1973. Molly's quick thinking saves her and her sisters from a threatening giant.

Read Aloud

Aardema, Verna. *Tales from the Story Hat.* New York: Coward, McCann, 1960. Ten witty pourquoi tales from Africa.

Arkhurst, Joyce Cooper. *The Adventures of Spider.* Boston: Little, Brown & Co., 1964. Includes the tale "Why Spider Has a Bald Head."

Buck, Pearl S. *The Chinese Story Teller.* New York: John Day Co., 1971. A cat and a dog vie for their master's attention. A pourquoi tale that explains why dogs chase cats.

Hoban, Russell C. *La Corona and the Tin Frog.* New York: Jonathan Cape, 1981. These four poignant stories, similar to tales by Anderson, are linked by the setting, a child's toy-filled nursery.

Lobel, Arnold. *Fables.* New York: Harper & Row, 1980. This collection of contemporary fables contains tales about such unlikely animals as a camel who wishes to dance, a mouse who dreams of the sea, and a crocodile dazzled by his wallpaper.

Related Media

The following key is used to identify the media listed below: **C**—cassette; **F**—film; **FS**—filmstrip; **R**—record. The catalog number immediately following each title should be used when ordering from the company identified in the entry.

King, Carole. *Really Rosie.* Ode Records, 1975. **R**

The Magic Porridge Pot. JFS 180 Old Greenwich, CT: Listening Library. **FS** with cassette.

The Heart of the Woods

HARCOURT BRACE JOVANOVICH, PUBLISHERS
Orlando   New York   Chicago   San Diego   Atlanta   Dallas

The Heart of the Woods

ODYSSEY An HBJ Literature Program

The title of this book is from the poem "Heart of the Woods" by Wesley Curtright on page 188.

Sam Leaton Sebesta

Consultants

Elaine M. Aoki   Carolyn Horovitz

Willard E. Bill   Myra Cohn Livingston

Sonya Blackman   Daphne P. Muse

Sylvia Engdahl   Barre Toelken

ISBN 0–15–333353–7

Acknowledgments

For permission to reprint copyrighted material, grateful acknowledgment is made to the following sources:

Atheneum Publishers, Inc.: ''We Could Be Friends'' from *The Way Things Are and Other Poems* by Myra Cohn Livingston (A Margaret K. McElderry Book). Copyright © 1974 by Myra Cohn Livingston. From *Oh, A-Hunting We Will Go* by John Langstaff (A Margaret K. McElderry Book). Text copyright © 1974 by John Langstaff. ''Spinning Song'' from *Today Is Saturday* by Zilpha Keatley Snyder. Text copyright © 1969 Zilpha Keatley Snyder. ''Something Is There'' and ''We Three'' from *See My Lovely Poison Ivy* by Lilian Moore. Text copyright © 1975 by Lilian Moore.

Bradbury Press, Inc., Scarsdale, New York: From *Rrra-ah* by Eros Keith. Copyright © 1969 by Eros Keith.

Shirley Crawford: First 8 lines from ''Grandfather'' by Shirley Crawford, © 1968 by Shirley Crawford.

Thomas Y. Crowell: ''Rope Rhyme'' from *Honey, I Love: and Other Love Poems* by Eloise Greenfield. Copyright © 1978 by Eloise Greenfield. ''Snowflakes drift'' from *I See the Winds* by Kazue Mizumura. Copyright © 1966 by Kazue Mizumura. ''Dilly Dilly Piccalilli'' from *Father Fox's Pennyrhymes* by Clyde Watson. Text copyright © 1971 by Clyde Watson.

Delacorte Press/Seymour Lawrence: ''Sebastian and the Monster'' excerpted from the book *Journeys of Sebastian* by Fernando Krahn. Copyright © 1968 by Fernando Krahn. Reprinted by permission of Delacorte Press/Seymour Lawrence.

The Dial Press: ''He wears a wooden shirt'' and ''When they stand'' excerpted from the book *Three Rolls and One Doughnut: Fables from Russia* retold by Mirra Ginsburg. Copyright © 1970 by Mirra Ginsburg.

Ernesto Galarza: ''Frog,'' ''Earthworm,'' and ''Bee'' from *Poemas Pe-que Pe-que Pe-que-nitos (Very Very Short Nature Poems)* by Ernesto Galarza.

Harper & Row, Publishers, Inc.: ''Grandfather's Story'' (retitled) adapted from *Little Bear's Visit* by Else Holmelund Minarik, illustrated by Maurice Sendak. Copyright © 1961 by Else Holmelund Minarik. Pictures copyright © 1961 by Maurice Sendak. ''The Garden'' from *Frog and Toad Together* written and illustrated by Arnold Lobel. Copyright © 1971, 1972 by Arnold Lobel. Adapted from *Dinosaur Time* by Peggy Parish. Text copyright © 1974 by Margaret Parish. ''Heart of the Woods'' by Wesley Curtright in *Golden Slippers* edited by Arna Bontemps. Copyright 1941 by Harper & Row, Publishers, Inc. *Pierre: A Cautionary Tale in Five Chapters and a Prologue,* written and illustrated by Maurice Sendak. Copyright © 1962 by Maurice Sendak. Adaptation of text of *Crystal Is the New Girl* by Shirley Gordon. Text copyright © 1976 by Shirley Gordon.

Holt, Rinehart and Winston, Publishers: ''January'' (retitled) from *Everett Anderson's Year* by Lucille Clifton. Copyright © 1974 by Lucille Clifton.

Houghton Mifflin Company: ''Split Pea Soup'' from *George and Martha* by James Marshall. Copyright © 1972 by James Marshall.

J. B. Lippincott Company: ''Fire! Fire!'' from *Fun in American Folk Rhymes* by Ray Wood. Copyright 1952 by Ray Wood.

Macmillan Publishing Co., Inc.: Reprinted from *Max* by Rachel Isadora. Copyright © 1976 by Rachel Isadora. ''Soft Grass'' from *Green Light, Go,* A Bank Street Reader, Revised Edition by Bank Street College of Education. Copyright © 1966, 1972 Macmillan Publishing Co., Inc.

Eve Merriam, c/o International Creative Management: ''Alarm Clock'' from *Finding a Poem* by Eve Merriam. Copyright © 1970 by Eve Merriam.

National Textbook Company: ''Caballito'' from *Mother Goose on the Rio Grande* by Frances Alexander. Copyright © 1973 by National Textbook Company.

Random House, Inc.: ''The Trolls and the Pussy Cat'' adapted from *Favorite Tales of Monsters and Trolls,* by George Jonsen. Copyright © 1977 by Random House, Inc. ''The Ant and the Dove'' from *Aesop's Fables,* retold by Anne Terry White. Copyright © 1964 by Anne Terry White.

Schroder Music Company (ASCAP): From the song: ''You Can't Make a Turtle Come Out.'' Words and music by Malvina Reynolds from *There's Music in the Air.* © Copyright 1962 by Schroder Music Co.

Charles Scribner's Sons: ''At the Top of My Voice'' from *At*

Art Acknowledgments

Contents

10

1 Tell Me Something Very Silly

Dilly Dilly Piccalilli

A rhyme by Clyde Watson

Objectives ● To enjoy humor and word play in nonsense verses. ● To make up nonsense rhymes.

Introducing the Poems   *What is the silliest thing you've ever seen? Your textbook begins with two very silly poems. Let's read them.*
Words to Know
   chap: a man or boy. (page 12)
      sausage: ground meat, usually in a thin tube or skin. (page 13)
Discussion Questions   *Tell me two silly things that happened in the poems. (Bert ate the buttons off his shirt; sausages danced.) What is funny about the title of the second rhyme? ("Saw such" is spelled "sausage.")*

Dilly Dilly Piccalilli

Tell me something very silly:

There was a chap his name was Bert

He ate the buttons off his shirt.

Who Ever Sausage a Thing?

A rhyme

Enriching Activities   **1.** *Nonsense rhymes.*
Have the children make up new silly endings
to "Dilly Dilly Piccalilli." To begin this activity,
give the class an example of a new ending:

One day a girl went walking

And went into a store;

She bought a pound of sausages

And laid them on the floor.

The girl began to whistle

A merry little tune—

And all the little sausages

Danced around the room!

"There was a girl her name was Sue/She
drank her milk from her right shoe."   **2.** *Improvisation.* Read the second poem aloud
while the children pretend to be sausages
and rise to dance around the room.

Pictures by Dora Leder

Objectives ● To consider reasons for a character's behavior in a story. ● To infer reasons for a change in a character's attitude. ● To interpret a humorous tale through Readers Theatre.

Reading Level Average

Synopsis of the Story Pierre only says "I don't care" to all of his parents' suggestions. Annoyed by his indifference, they leave him at home alone. When a hungry lion appears and proposes to eat him, Pierre still responds, "I don't care." Pierre ends up in the lion's stomach until his parents and a doctor rescue him. Happy to be alive, Pierre decides that he does indeed care.

PIERRE

a cautionary tale
IN
FIVE CHAPTERS
AND A
PROLOGUE

A *cautionary tale* is a story that has a warning in it.

Story and pictures
by Maurice Sendak

Prologue

Tell the children that a *prologue* introduces a story.

There once was a boy
named Pierre
who only would say,
"I don't care!"
Read his story,
my friend,
for you'll find
at the end
that a suitable
moral lies there.

Suitable means *proper* or *fitting*.

14

Introducing the Story   *This is a story about a boy who says the same thing to everybody. I wonder if you have ever said what Pierre always says. Let's find out what happens when he says it once too often!*

Words to Know
  moral: the lesson of a story. (page 14)
  shock: a sudden, strong upset of the mind or feelings. (page 26)
  guest: a person entertained by others. (page 30)

Chapter 1

Explain that each *chapter* in the story tells about a different event.

One day
his mother said
when Pierre
climbed out of bed,
"Good morning,
darling boy,
you are
my only joy."
Pierre said,
"I don't care!"

"What would you
like to eat?"
"I don't care!"
"Some lovely
cream of wheat?"
"I don't care!"
"Don't sit backwards
on your chair."
"I don't care!"
"Or pour syrup
on your hair."
"I don't care!"

"You are acting
like a clown."
"I don't care!"
"And we have
to go to town."
"I don't care!"
"Don't you want
to come, my dear?"
"I don't care!"
"Would you rather
stay right here?"
"I don't care!"

So his mother
left him there.

Chapter 2

His father said,
"Get off your head
or I will march you
up to bed!"
Pierre said,
"I don't care!"
"I would think
that you could see—"
"I don't care!"
"Your head is where
your feet should be!"
"I don't care!"

"If you keep standing
upside down—"
"I don't care!"
"We'll never ever
get to town."
"I don't care!"
"If only you would
say I CARE."
"I don't care!"
"I'd let you fold
the folding chair."
"I don't care!"

So his parents
left him there.
They didn't take him
anywhere.

Chapter 3

Now, as the night
began to fall
a hungry lion
paid a call.
He looked Pierre
right in the eye
and asked him
if he'd like to die.
Pierre said,
"I don't care!"

"I can eat you,
don't you see?"
"I don't care!"
"And you will be
inside of me."
"I don't care!"
"Then you'll never
have to bother—"
"I don't care!"
"With a mother
and a father."
"I don't care!"

"Is that all
you have to say?"
"I don't care!"
"Then I'll eat you,
if I may."
"I don't care!"

So the lion
ate Pierre.

Chapter 4

Arriving home
at six o'clock,
his parents had
a dreadful shock!
They found the lion
sick in bed
and cried,
"Pierre is surely dead!"

They pulled the lion
by the hair.
They hit him
with the folding chair.
His mother asked,
"Where is Pierre?"
The lion answered,
"I don't care!"
His father said,
"Pierre's in there!"

Chapter 5

They rushed the lion
into town.
The doctor shook him
up and down.
And when the lion
gave a roar—
Pierre fell out
upon the floor.
He rubbed his eyes
and scratched his head
and laughed
because he wasn't dead.

His mother cried
and held him tight.
His father asked,
"Are you all right?"
Pierre said,
"I am feeling fine,
please take me home,
it's half past nine."
The lion said,
"If you would care
to climb on me,
I'll take you there."
Then everyone
looked at Pierre
who shouted,
"*Yes, indeed I care!!*"

Half past nine is
another way to say
9:30.

The lion took them
home to rest
and stayed on
as a weekend guest.

The moral of Pierre
is: CARE!

Discussion Questions   *What did Pierre learn at the end of the story?* (To care.) *Why did Pierre finally care?* (Possible answers: he was glad to be out of the lion; he wanted the lion to take him home.)

Enriching Activities   1. *Readers Theatre.* Choose children to play the characters in *Pierre* and have a good reader be the narrator. Have the children perform the story using the Readers Theatre techniques on page T41.   **2.** *Music/singing.* Have the children listen to Carole King's song "Pierre" from the record *Really Rosie* (Ode Records, 1975). Tell the children to sing along with the record when Pierre says, "I don't care."

Questions

1. Tell at least one thing that Pierre did before the lion came.

2. Why was the lion sick?

3. Pierre's father said, "Pierre's in there." How did he know?

4. If you "pay a call," what do you do?
      visit   shout   buy

5. Who helped Pierre to care?

1. Literal/recall He sat backward on his chair (page 16); poured syrup in his hair (page 16); acted like a clown (page 17); stood on his head (page 19).
2. Interpretive/ inference   He had eaten Pierre. (page 26)
3. Interpretive/ inference   Like Pierre, the lion said, "I don't care." (page 27)
4. Vocabulary   Visit. (page 22)
5. Interpretive/ inference   The lion.

Activity

Pierre, why did you always say, "I don't care"? Help Pierre answer. Write what he might say.

Interpretive/extra- polation   *Point-of- view writing.* Encourage the children to answer from Pierre's point of view. They may say that Pierre was in a bad mood or did not want to go to town.

About MAURICE SENDAK

Did anyone ever tell stories to you when you were sick? As a boy, Maurice Sendak was sick for a very long time. During that time, his father made up stories for him and his brother and sister.

When he was nine, Maurice Sendak began writing his own stories. He often hand-lettered the stories and drew pictures to go with them. When he was older, he spent many hours at his window drawing the children playing outside. One of the children was a girl named Rosie.

Many years later, Maurice Sendak wrote a book about Rosie called *The Sign on Rosie's Door.* He has written and illustrated many other stories as well that people of all ages enjoy.

More Books by Maurice Sendak

Higglety Pigglety Pop! or There Must Be More to Life   (Harper & Row, 1967)
Where the Wild Things Are   (Harper & Row, 1963)
The Nutshell Library   (Harper & Row, 1962)

What Can They Be?

Two riddles from Russia retold by Mirra Ginsburg

Objectives ● To enjoy riddles from other countries. ● To write riddles.
Introducing the Riddles *Look carefully at the pictures on this page as you try to solve these two riddles from Russia. The riddles are about objects very familiar to you.*

He wears a wooden shirt,

And his nose is dark.

Wherever he goes,

He leaves a mark.

(A pencil.)

When they are empty, they stand,

When they are full, they walk.

(Shoes.)

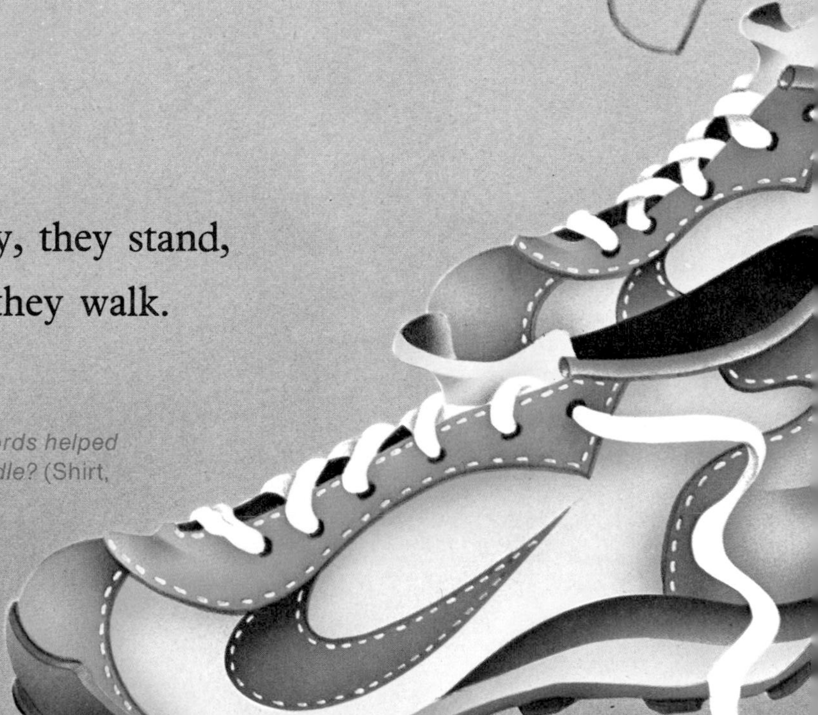

Discussion Question *What words helped you guess the answer to each riddle?* (Shirt, nose, mark; stand and walk.)

Enriching Activity *Writing riddles.* Have the children write riddles about objects used in school; for example, desks, books, paper. Tell them to write at least two sentences describing the object. Their riddles should end with the question "What is it?"

Picture by Sharon Harker

Oh, A-Hunting We Will Go

An old song with new verses by John Langstaff and friends

Oh, a-hunting we will go,
A-hunting we will go,
We'll catch a fox
And put it in a box,
And then we'll let it go!

Pictures by Marie-Louise Gay

Objectives ● To enjoy an old song. ● To recognize rhyme and rhythm patterns in a song.
Introducing the Song *Here is an old song that you have probably heard, but some of the verses may be new to you.*

Words to Know
bunk: a narrow bed. (page 36)
brontosaurus: a large plant-eating dinosaur. (page 37)
chorus: a group of singers who perform together. (page 37)

Oh, a-hunting we will go,
A-hunting we will go,
We'll catch a goat
And put it in a boat,
And then we'll let it go!

35

Oh, a-hunting we will go,
A-hunting we will go,
We'll catch a skunk
And put it in a bunk,
And then we'll let it go!

Discussion Question *Name two things in the song that you probably wouldn't do.* (Put a skunk in a bunk; put a brontosaurus in a chorus.)

Enriching Activities **1.** *Rhyming/cut-paper art.* Have the children make up rhymes following the song pattern. To begin the activity, have them draw or paste pictures of animals on paper. Then tell the children to write out the song's verse, adding two rhyming lines about their animals. Give this example: "We'll catch a cat/And put it in a hat." **2.** *Singing.* Teach the melody of the song to the children. The music is on page T58.

Oh, a-hunting we will go,

A-hunting we will go,

We'll catch a brontosaurus

And put it in a chorus,

And then we'll let it go!

37

Solomon Grundy

A Mother Goose rhyme retold by Frederick Winsor

Objectives ● To recognize chronological order in a rhyme. ● To compare two versions of a rhyme. ● To make up new sequences to the rhyme.

Solomon Grundy
Walked on Monday
Rode on Tuesday
Motored Wednesday
Planed on Thursday
Rocketed Friday
Spaceship Saturday
Time Machine Sunday
Where is the end for
Solomon Grundy?

Explain that a *time machine* (line 8) is a fantasy invention that allows travel into the past and the future.

Picture by Jim M'Guiness

Introducing the Rhyme *"Solomon Grundy" is an old Mother Goose rhyme, but a poet has written it in a new way. I'll read the old rhyme first. (The rhyme is on page T57.) Now let's read the new rhyme to see how it has changed.*

Discussion Questions *How are the two Solomon Grundy rhymes alike?* (They are about the same person; both are arranged by the days of the week.) *How is the new rhyme different?* (It is about methods of travel, not about lifetime activities; it has an unanswered question at the end.)

Enriching Activities **1.** *Creative thinking.* Have the children suggest other activities for Solomon Grundy. Choose a topic such as playground games: plays hopscotch Monday, swings on Tuesday, and so on. **2.** *Pantomime.* Ask volunteers to pantomime Solomon Grundy's activities. Have the children guess what Solomon is doing.

39

"Fire! Fire!"

A rhyme

"Fire! Fire!"

Cried Mrs. McGuire.

"Where! Where!"

Cried Mrs. Blair.

"All over town!"

Cried Mrs. Brown.

"Get some water!"

Cried Mrs. Carter.

"We'd better jump!"

Cried Mrs. Gump.

"That would be silly!"

Cried Mrs. Brunelli.

"It looks too risky!"

Cried Mrs. Matruski.

"What'll we do?"

Cried Mrs. LaRue.

"Turn in an alarm!"

Cried Mrs. Storm.

"Save us! Save us!"

Cried Mrs. Davis.

The fire department got the call
And the firemen saved them, one and all.

1. *Choral reading.* Pick children to play the characters in the rhyme. Then have the children say the characters' lines while the class reads the rest of the rhyme. Encourage the children to use expressive voices and gestures. **2.** *Class verse.* Have the children write a class verse following the "Fire! Fire!" rhyme pattern. Help them choose a situation for their rhymes; a sudden rainstorm, for example, might inspire the rhymes " 'Rain! Rain!'/Cried Mrs. Pane" and " 'Get inside!'/Cried Mrs. Hyde." Write the rhymes on the board.

The Garden

Story and pictures by Arnold Lobel

Objectives ● To recognize the humor in a misunderstanding. ● To predict what will happen next. ● To interpret a story through Story Theater.

Synopsis of the Story After admiring Frog's garden, Toad plants some seeds. When they do not immediately sprout, Toad decides they are afraid to grow and tries to comfort them with candles, stories, and songs. Toad becomes tired and falls asleep. When he awakens, his plants are growing. Toad is happy, but he agrees with Frog that having a garden is hard work.

Background The story "The Garden" appears in the book *Frog and Toad Together,* a Newbery Honor Book in 1973.

Introducing the Story *Have you ever been so hungry that you thought your lunchtime would never come? If you want something to happen right away, it usually seems to take much longer than you thought it would. In this story, Toad is very impatient for his garden to grow, and he does some very funny things to hurry it along.*

Frog was in his garden.

Toad came walking by.

"What a fine garden
you have, Frog," he said.

"Yes," said Frog. "It is very nice,
but it was hard work."

"I wish I had a garden," said Toad.

"Here are some flower seeds.
Plant them in the ground," said Frog,
"and soon you will have a garden."

"How soon?" asked Toad.

"Quite soon," said Frog.

Toad ran home.

He planted the flower seeds.

"Now, seeds," said Toad,
"start growing."

Toad walked up and down
a few times.

The seeds did not start to grow.

Toad put his head
close to the ground
and said loudly, "Now, seeds,
start growing!"
Toad looked at the ground again.
The seeds did not start to grow.

Toad put his head
very close to the ground and shouted,
"NOW, SEEDS, START GROWING!"
　　Frog came running up the path.
　　"What is all this noise?" he asked.
　　"My seeds will not grow," said Toad.
　　"You are shouting too much,"
said Frog. "These poor seeds
are afraid to grow."
　　"My seeds are afraid to grow?"
asked Toad.

"Of course," said Frog.
"Leave them alone for a few days.
Let the sun shine on them,
let the rain fall on them.
Soon your seeds will start to grow."

That night Toad looked out
of his window.

"Drat!" said Toad. "My seeds
have not started to grow.
They must be afraid of the dark."

Toad went out to his garden
with some candles.

"I will read the seeds a story,"
said Toad. "Then they will not
be afraid."

Toad read a long story
to his seeds.

All the next day
Toad sang songs
to his seeds.

And all the next day
Toad read poems
to his seeds.

And all the next day
Toad played music
for his seeds.

Toad looked at the ground.
The seeds still did not
start to grow.

"What shall I do?"
cried Toad. "These must be
the most frightened seeds
in the whole world!"

Then Toad felt very tired,
and he fell asleep.

"Toad, Toad, wake up," said Frog.
"Look at your garden!"

Toad looked at his garden.
Little green plants were coming up
out of the ground.

"At last," shouted Toad,
"my seeds have stopped
being afraid to grow!"

"And now you will have
a nice garden too," said Frog.

"Yes," said Toad,
"but you were right, Frog.
It was very hard work."

Discussion Question *If Toad plants a garden next year, what do you think he will do to make the seeds grow?* (Possible answer: the same things, because he doesn't know how plants grow.)
Enriching Activities 1. *Story Theater.* Select children to play the parts of Frog, Toad, and the plants. Have a few children read the story while others improvise the action. The children playing the plants could pretend to be afraid or very sleepy at first. Suggest that they open their arms and hands when the seeds sprout stems and leaves. See page T42 for Story Theater techniques.
2. *Growing seeds.* Have the children plant seeds in three containers. Water two containers; put one in a sunny place and the other in a dark place. Put the dry container in a dark place. Ask the children to predict what will happen. Check the containers in a week.

1. Literal/recall
''Let the sun shine on them; let the rain fall on them.'' (page 47)
2. Literal/recall
He shouted (page 46); read stories and poems (pages 49–50); sang (page 50); played music (page 50).
3. Critical/relating to experience Possible answers: water them; pull weeds; hoe the earth around them.
4. Vocabulary and Interpretive/inference ''Right away.'' (page 43)
5. Vocabulary and Interpretive/inference ''A few days.'' (page 43)

Questions

1. Frog told Toad how to make seeds grow. Tell two things Frog said.

2. Toad did funny things to make his seeds grow. Tell what Toad did.

3. How would *you* make seeds grow?

4. Frog said Toad's seeds would come up ''quite soon.'' What did ''quite soon'' mean to Toad?

5. What did Frog mean by ''quite soon''?

Interpretive/extrapolation *Story extension.* The funny surprises in the stories may be realistic, such as ''Huge weeds grew in the garden'' or fanciful, such as ''The plants became musical instruments.''

Activity

Write what happened after the seeds came up in Toad's garden. Show what happened with a picture. Put a funny surprise in your story and picture.

BOOKSHELF

A Great Big Ugly Man Came Up and Tied His Horse to Me: A Book of Nonsense Verse. Pictures by Wallace Tripp. Little, Brown, 1973. This book has many silly rhymes, old and new. The pictures are as funny as the rhymes.   **Reading Level** Average

Riddle Rat by Donald Hall. Warne, 1977. Riddle Rat guesses the answers to all Aunt Agatha's riddles. Soon he is making up his own riddles.   **Reading Level** Average

Old Mother Hubbard and Her Dog. Pictures by Evaline Ness. Holt, Rinehart and Winston, 1972. Mother Hubbard can't make her dog happy in this rhyme.   **Reading Level** Easy

The Great Big Enormous Turnip by Alexei Tolstoy. Franklin Watts, 1968. An old man and an old woman cannot pull up an enormous turnip in their garden. Their granddaughter, the dog, the cat, and even the mouse come to help.   **Reading Level** Average

Lambs for Dinner by Betsy Maestro. Crown, 1978. A hungry wolf invites a family of lambs to dinner. The menu is a surprise.   **Reading Level** Challenging

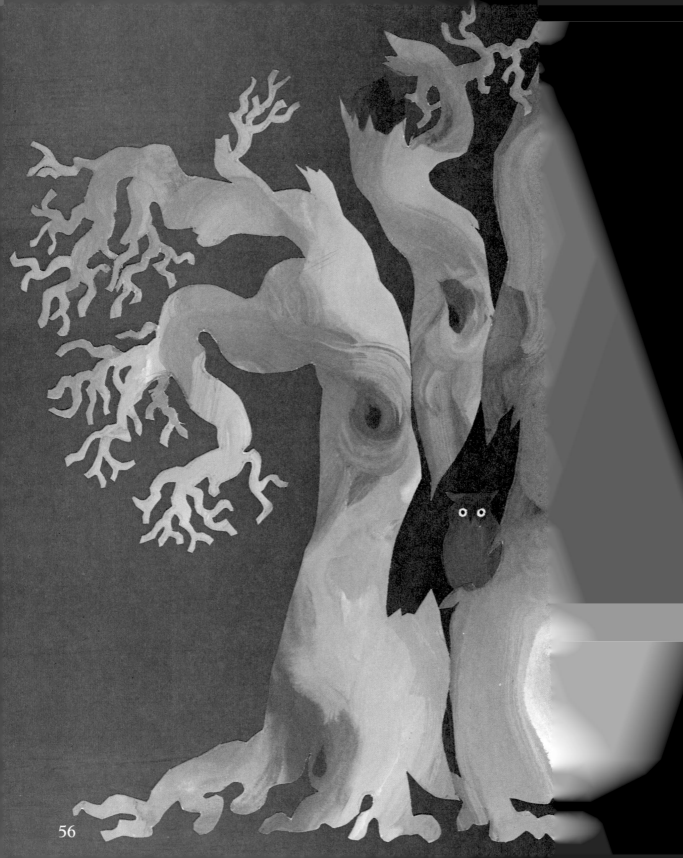

2 Something Is There

Teeny-Tiny

An English folk tale

retold by Joseph Jacobs

Pictures by Stephen Osborn

Reading Level Average

Once upon a time
there was a teeny-tiny woman
who lived in a teeny-tiny house
in a teeny-tiny town.

Now one day this teeny-tiny woman
put on her teeny-tiny bonnet
and went out of her teeny-tiny house
to take a teeny-tiny walk. *A bonnet is a kind of hat.*

And when this teeny-tiny woman
had gone a teeny-tiny way,
she came to a teeny-tiny gate.
So the teeny-tiny woman
opened the teeny-tiny gate
and went into a teeny-tiny churchyard.

And when this teeny-tiny woman
had got into the teeny-tiny churchyard,
she saw a teeny-tiny bone.
The teeny-tiny woman
said to her teeny-tiny self,
"This teeny-tiny bone
will make me some teeny-tiny soup
for my teeny-tiny supper."

59

So the teeny-tiny woman
put the teeny-tiny bone
into her teeny-tiny pocket
and went home to her teeny-tiny house.

Now when the teeny-tiny woman
got home to her teeny-tiny house,
she was a teeny-tiny bit tired.
So she went up her teeny-tiny stairs
to her teeny-tiny bed
and put the teeny-tiny bone
into a teeny-tiny cupboard.

And when this teeny-tiny woman
had been asleep a teeny-tiny time,
she was awakened by a teeny-tiny voice
from the teeny-tiny cupboard,
that said,

"Give me my bone!"

And this teeny-tiny woman
was a teeny-tiny bit frightened.
So she hid her teeny-tiny head
under the teeny-tiny covers
and went to sleep again.

And when she had been asleep again
a teeny-tiny time,
the teeny-tiny voice again
cried out from the teeny-tiny cupboard
a teeny-tiny louder,

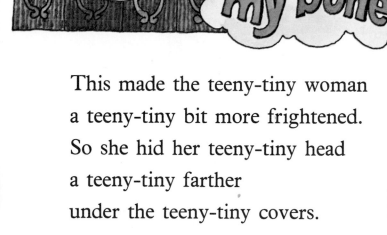

Give me
my bone!

This made the teeny-tiny woman
a teeny-tiny bit more frightened.
So she hid her teeny-tiny head
a teeny-tiny farther
under the teeny-tiny covers.

Discussion Question *What words are repeated throughout the story? (Teeny-tiny.)*

Enriching Activities **1.** *Painting.* Have the children paint what said, "Give me my bone!" **2.** *Related reading.* Read Lilian Moore's poem "Teeny Tiny Ghost" to the class. The poem is on page T58.

And when the teeny-tiny woman

had been asleep again

a teeny-tiny time,

the teeny-tiny voice

from the teeny-tiny cupboard

said again a teeny-tiny louder,

"Give me my bone!"

And this teeny-tiny woman

was a teeny-tiny bit more frightened.

But she put her teeny-tiny head

out of the teeny-tiny covers

and said in her loudest teeny-tiny voice,

Something Is There

A poem by Lilian Moore

Something is there
there on the stair
coming down
coming down
stepping with care.
Coming down
coming down
slinkety-sly.

Something is coming and wants to get by.

Picture by Kinuko Craft

Grandfather's Story

From the story *Little Bear's Visit* by Else Holmelund Minarik

Pictures by Maurice Sendak

"Grandfather," asked Little Bear,
"how about a goblin story?"

"Yes, if you will hold my paw,"
said Grandfather.

"I will not be scared," said Little Bear.

"No," said Grandfather Bear.
"But I may be scared."

"Oh, Grandfather! Begin the story."

So Grandfather began.

One day a little goblin
went by an old cave.
It was old,
it was cold,
it was dark.

And something inside it went bump.

What was that?

BUMP!

"Hoo—ooh——" cried the goblin.

He got so scared that he jumped
right out of his shoes.
Then he began to run.

Pit—pat—pit—pat—pit—pat——
What was that?
SOMETHING was running after him.

Oh, my goodness, what could it be?
The goblin was too scared to look back.
He ran faster than ever.
But so did the SOMETHING that went
pit—pat—pit—pat—pit—pat——

The goblin saw a hole in a tree.
He jumped inside to hide.
The pit–pat–pit–pat came closer,
closer — CLOSER — till it stopped,
right by the hole in the tree!

Then all was quiet.
Nothing happened.
Nothing.

To *peek* is to look secretly or quickly at something.

The little goblin wanted to peek out.

It was so quiet.

Should he peek out?

Yes, he would. He WOULD peek out!

And he did.

"Eeeeeh——!" cried the goblin.

Do you know what he saw?

He saw—his SHOES!
His own little shoes
——and nothing more.
"Goodness," said the goblin,
hopping out of the tree.

"That old bump in the cave
made me jump right out of my shoes.
But they came running after me,
didn't they!
And here they are!"

He picked up his shoes,
hugged them,
and put them back on.

"Good little shoes," said the goblin.
"You didn't want to stay behind,
did you!" He laughed.
"Who cares about an old bump,
anyway," he said.
So he snapped his fingers,
and skipped away——

"——just like that!" said Grandfather.

"I can't jump out of my shoes,"
said Little Bear,
"because I don't have any."
He chuckled. "That's how I like it."

To *chuckle* is to laugh
softly.

Discussion Questions *What do you think went* bump? (Encourage imaginative as well as realistic answers.) *Who tells you stories? What kinds of stories do you like? Everybody gets scared sometimes. What do you do when you are scared of something?* (Possible answer: I talk to my parents about it.)

Enriching Activity *Point-of-view writing.* Have the children pretend they are the goblin's shoes and write an answer to the question, ''Shoes, why did you follow the goblin?'' Some children might answer that the shoes were also afraid or that they were lonely.

1. Literal/recall He held it so Grandfather would not be afraid; or **Interpretive/ inference** Grandfather was pretending to be afraid. (page 65)
2. Literal/recall He jumped out of his shoes and ran away. (page 67)
3. Interpretive/ inference He was glad that they, and not something frightening, had followed him; or **Literal/recall** he was glad to see them (page 72)

Questions

1. Why did Little Bear hold Grandfather's paw?

2. What did the goblin do when he heard the BUMP?

3. Why did the goblin hug his shoes?

4. Which is a good place to hide?
   a cave   a goblin   shoes

4. Vocabulary
A cave. (page 66)

Activity

It is night. You are walking down the street. You hear THUMP, THUMP behind you. Draw a picture to show what made the THUMP, THUMP. Write a sentence to tell what you would do.

Interpretive/extrapolation *Story writing/ drawing.* The children may want to write about imaginary creatures, such as ghosts, or realistic ones, such as a dog or a cat.

About ELSE HOLMELUND MINARIK

A little girl wanted to read
when she was still very young.
So her mother wrote books
for her. A class of first graders
did not have books to read
during the summer. So their
teacher wrote some stories
for them.

That mother and teacher
is the same person. Her name
is Else Holmelund Minarik.
The books she wrote are
called the *Little Bear* books,
and you can still enjoy her stories about Little
Bear, his family, and his friends.

More Books by Else Holmelund Minarik

A Kiss for Little Bear   (Harper & Row, 1968)

Little Bear's Visit   (Harper & Row, 1961)

No Fighting, No Biting   (Harper & Row, 1958)

Cat and Dog   (Harper & Row, 1960)

The Little Giant Girl and the Elf Boy   (Harper & Row, 1963)

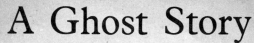

A Ghost Story

A Japanese rhyme

Objectives   ● To identify the question and answer structure in a rhyme.   ● To make comparisons between unlike objects.
Introducing the Rhyme   *Have you ever looked at an object and thought it was something else? This rhyme asks a question about such a moment, but you may be surprised by the answer.*

"Hello, you, are you a ghost,
Hiding there behind that post?"

"No, I'm just an old dead tree—
You needn't be afraid of me."

Word to Know
   post: an upright piece of wood or other
      material.
Discussion Questions   *What is the question in the poem?* ("Are you a ghost?") *What is the answer in the poem?* ("No, I'm just an old dead tree.")
Enriching Activities   1. *Comparisons/ drawing.* Ask the class to name objects they see every day, such as fences, grass, and clouds. Then have the children draw sketches of what they might imagine the objects to be. The children may see clouds, for example, and imagine woolly sheep; they might see a kitten and imagine a powder puff.   **2.** *Oral extension.* Divide the class into pairs. Have one child in each pair choose an object in the classroom and ask it a question like that in the poem. The partner should respond as the object; for example, "No, I am just an eraser—/You needn't be afraid of me."

Picture by Kinuko Craft

Sebastian and the Monster

A picture story by Fernando Krahn

See page T48 for an article that contains general information about wordless picture books and specific suggestions for using them in the classroom.

Objectives ● To recognize that pictures can tell a story. ● To interpret a wordless picture story.

Synopsis of the Story Sebastian pulls on a string hanging from a hole in the wall, and discovers that it is the tail of a monster. As soon as Sebastian climbs onto the monster's back, four riders on similar monsters begin a race. Sebastian crosses the finish line first. The monster climbs into the winner's trophy and disappears.

Introducing the Story *Some very surprising things happen when Sebastian pulls on a string hanging from a hole. Enjoy this picture story as you tell it to yourself. It's a monstrously exciting tale!*

Ask what the monsters have on their heads
(numbers). When the monsters begin racing,
ask why the numbers are useful (the winner
will be easy to identify).

84

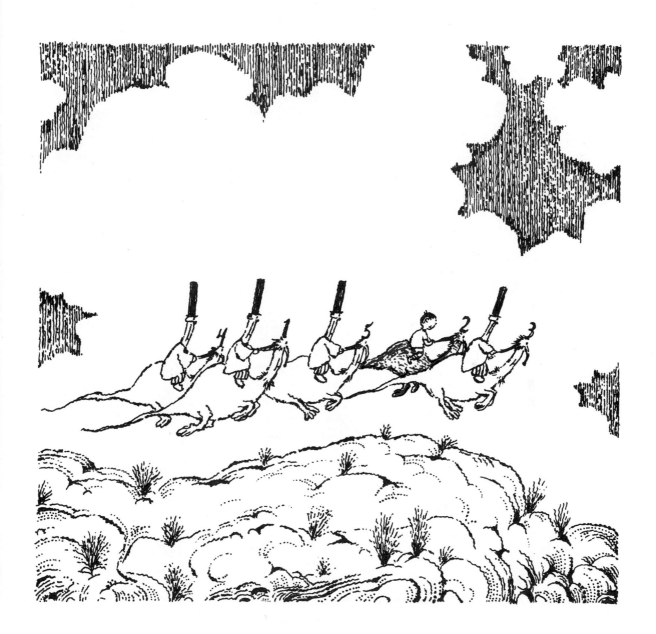

Discussion Questions *How could the story have ended if the monster had not been friendly?* (Possible answers: the monster could have eaten Sebastian; it could have taken the trophy.) *What do you think Sebastian is thinking about in the last picture?* (Possible answers: he is wondering where the monster went; he is admiring the trophy.)

Enriching Activities **1.** *Storytelling.* Make a tape recording of the Sebastian story. Choose children to tell what is happening in each picture. Encourage them to name the characters and make up conversations between them. When they finish, play the tape as the children look at the story again.

2. *Monster book.* Have the children draw and name their own friendly monsters. Tell them to use the rest of the paper to write words describing their monsters, such as *soft, speedy, huge,* and *cuddly.* Make a construction-paper cover for the drawings, and entitle the book ''The Friendly Monster Book.''

We Three

A poem by Lilian Moore

Objectives ● To enjoy the surprise ending of a poem. ● To respond to the subject of a poem by writing a story.

Introducing the Poem *Halloween is always a mysterious time. This poem tells about a very strange thing that happened one Halloween night!*
Discussion Question *What strange thing happened in the poem?* (Possible answers: a monster joined the children; a child in costume joined them.)
Enriching Activities **1.** *Writing stories.* Have the children write stories about personal or imaginary Halloween adventures. **2.** *Role playing.* Ask volunteers to pantomime the roles of various Halloween characters, and have the class guess who they are pretending to be.

We three
went out on Halloween,
A Pirate
An Ape
A Witch between.

We went from door to door.

By the light
of the moon
these shadows were seen
A Pirate
An Ape
A Witch between
and—

Say, how did we get to be FOUR?

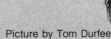

94   Picture by Tom Durfee

BOOKSHELF

The Funny Little Woman retold by Arlene
Mosel. E. P. Dutton, 1972. The funny little
woman likes to laugh. She even laughs
when a mean *oni* (monster) catches her.
Will her laughing save her? **Reading Level** Average

You're the Scaredy Cat by Mercer Mayer.
Parent's Magazine Press, 1974. Two
brothers camp out in the backyard one
night. The older brother tells a scary story
to frighten his younger brother. Both
brothers are scared, but only one is the
scaredy cat. **Reading Level** Easy

Moon Bear by Frank Asch. Charles Scribner's
Sons, 1978. Bear sees the moon growing
smaller every night. Is it going to
disappear? Whom can he tell? **Reading Level** Easy

The King's Monster by Carolyn Haywood.
William Morrow, 1980. Though the princess
Gabriella is old enough to be married, the
monster in her father's dungeon frightens
away any young men. **Reading Level** Challenging

3 I Can Do It!

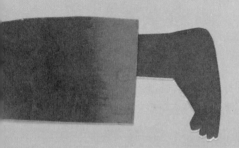

At the Top of My Voice

A poem by Felice Holman

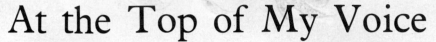

When I stamp
The ground thunders,
When I shout
The world rings,
When I sing
The air wonders
How I do such things.

Discussion Questions *What three things does the person in the poem do?* (Stamps; shouts; sings.) *What amazing things happen when she does these things?* (The ground thunders; the world rings; the air wonders.)
Enriching Activities **1.** *Creative thinking.* Have the children make up amazing things that could happen when they do something. Encourage them to follow the poem's pattern by exaggerating their stories; for example:

"When I whistle, the trees dance" or "When I kick a goal in soccer, the whole town cheers."
2. *Musical interpretation.* Have the children use sound effects during a rereading of the poem. Tell the class to stamp, shout, and sing at appropriate moments. Choose three children to give a musical interpretation of the effects in the poem, using a drum for the ground's "thunder," a triangle for the "ringing" world, and a xylophone or slide whistle for the "wondering" air.

Picture by Ronni Shepherd

Objectives • To infer reasons for change in a character's attitude. • To relate a story's main idea (theme) to personal experience. • To identify vocabulary relating to different activities.

Synopsis of the Story On Saturday mornings, Max walks his sister Lisa to her dancing school and then goes to the park to play baseball. One Saturday they are early, so Max visits the dancing school. Much to his surprise, he enjoys the class. He then goes to his game and hits a home run. Max decides that dancing is a great way to warm up for his Saturday baseball games.

Reading Level Average

MAX

Story and pictures by Rachel Isadora

Max is a great baseball player. He can run fast, jump high, and hardly ever misses a ball. Every Saturday he plays with his team in the park.

Introducing the Story *What sports do you like most? You should meet Max. He likes baseball more than anything, but he's never really tried other kinds of activities. Read Max's story to find out what happens when he tries something he thought he'd never like!*

Word to Know
  sneakers: rubber-soled canvas shoes, worn especially for sports. (page 106)

On Saturday mornings he walks with
his sister Lisa to her dancing school.
The school is on the way to the park.

One Saturday when they reach the school,
Max still has lots of time before
the game is to start. Lisa asks him
if he wants to come inside for a while.

Max doesn't really want to, but he says
O.K. Soon the class begins. He gets
a chair and sits near the door to watch.

The teacher invites Max
to join the class, but he must
take off his sneakers first.

Pronounced /bär/.
The *barre* (shown in
the top left picture of
the facing page) is a
handrail that dancers
use during practice.

In a *split* (shown in
the top right picture of
the facing page), one
is sitting on the floor
with legs stretched in
opposite directions.

Pronounced /pä′ də
shä′/. The children
in the picture at the
bottom of the facing
page are doing the
pas de chat. *Pas de
chat* is a French
phrase that means
step of a cat.

He stretches at the *barre*.   He tries to do the split.

And the *pas de chat*. He is having fun.

107

Just as the class lines up to do leaps
across the floor, Lisa points to the clock.
It is time for Max to leave.

Max doesn't want to miss the leaps.
He waits and takes his turn.

Then he must go.
He leaps all the way to the park.

He is late.

Everybody is waiting for him.

He goes up to bat.

Strike one!

He tries again.

Strike two!

And then . . .

A home run!

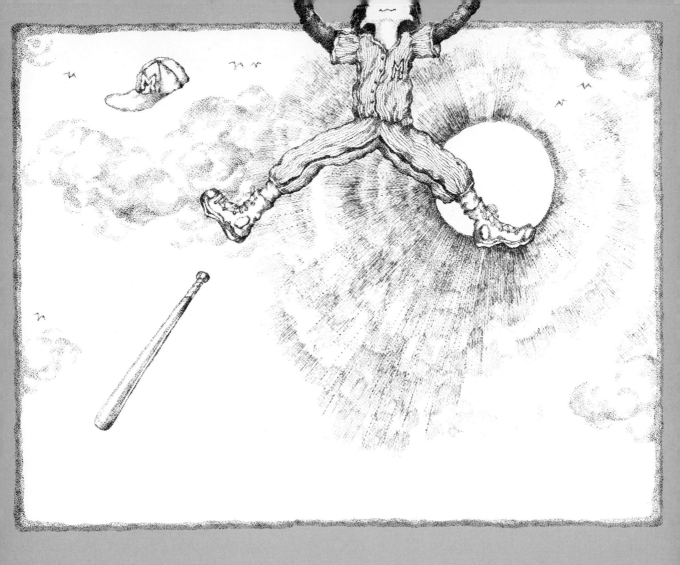

Now Max has a new way to warm up
for the game on Saturdays.
He goes to dancing class.

Discussion Questions *Why do you think Max didn't want to dance at first?* (Possible answer: he thought it was a "sissy" sport.) *What can you think of that you thought you wouldn't like, but liked when you tried it?* (Answers need not be limited to sports activities.)

Enriching Activity *Montage.* Discuss the story illustrations that show action. Then provide the children with a selection of sports and general-interest magazines. Have them cut out pictures of people engaged in a variety of activities, such as music, dancing, and sports. The children might paste their pictures on a large sheet of butcher paper and label the activities and the actions shown in each picture.

Questions

1. What did Max find out about dancing?

2. What exciting thing did Max do in the baseball game?

3. Tell what Max does on Saturdays now.

4. Someone says, "Baseball players don't dance." What does Max say?

5. Which three words in the story tell how dancers move?

1. Interpretive/ inference It was fun (page 107); it helped him warm up for baseball (page 116).

2. Literal/recall He hit a home run. (page 114)

3. Literal/recall He goes to dancing class, then plays baseball. (page 116)

4. Interpretive/ extrapolation He says that baseball players can also enjoy dancing.

5. Vocabulary Stretch (page 107); split (page 107); leap (page 108).

Activity **Critical/relating to experience** *Oral extension or writing.*

Max learned to do something new. He learned to dance. What new thing would you like to learn to do? Tell or write how you would try to learn to do it. Tell or write who might teach you.

117

Walk Tall in the World

A poem by Lucille Clifton

"Walk tall in the world,"
says Mama
to Everett Anderson.
"The year is new and
so are the days,
walk tall in the world,"
she says.

Picture by Carol Newsom

About LUCILLE CLIFTON

The mother of six children, Lucille Clifton writes poems and stories about children. She writes of what they like to do and how they feel: happy, sad, angry, proud.

Several of Lucille Clifton's books are about a boy named Everett Anderson. If you read them, you may discover you've done some of the things Everett Anderson has done. Maybe you and Everett Anderson sometimes feel the same way, too.

More Books by Lucille Clifton

Everett Anderson's Year   (Holt, Rinehart & Winston, 1974)

Everett Anderson's Friend   (Holt, Rinehart & Winston, 1976)

Everett Anderson's 1-2-3   (Holt, Rinehart & Winston, 1977)

My Brother Fine with Me   (Holt, Rinehart & Winston, 1975)

The Ant and the Dove

An Aesop fable retold by Anne Terry White   **Reading Level**   Challenging

Pictures by Christa Kieffer

A thirsty Ant was climbing down
a blade of grass that grew beside a
spring. She was trying to reach
the water so she could take a drink.
Unluckily she slipped and fell into
the spring.

Now a Dove was sitting on a branch over the water. She saw the Ant fall in and was filled with pity. Quick as a wink she pulled off a leaf and let it fall into the spring. The little raft settled down on the water right beside the drowning Ant. The Ant climbed on the leaf and was soon safe on shore again.

But what did she see? Hidden behind
a bush, a hunter was spreading his net.
He was going to catch the Dove!

"No!" the grateful Ant said. "You shall not take the bird that saved my life!" And with all her might she bit the hunter on his bare foot.

With a cry the hunter dropped his net, and the Dove flew away to the wood.

One good turn deserves another.

Explain that *might* means *strength* or *force.*

123

Reading Level Challenging

Mary Jo's Grandmother

Adapted from the story by Janice May Udry

Pictures by Charles Robinson

Introducing the Story *Have you ever helped someone who was very much in need of help? In this story, Mary Jo has to do some quick thinking when someone needs her. As we read, think what you might have done if you were Mary Jo.*

Words to Know
biscuits: a kind of bread baked in small, soft cakes. (page 129)
pantry: a room or a large closet where food and kitchen supplies are kept. (page 129)

Mary Jo's grandmother was quite old. She lived alone in a little house in the country.

Whenever Mary Jo's mother or father told Grandmother that she should move into town, Grandmother always said, "I've lived in this house almost all my life. I'm too old to move now. I'm happy here."

The family drove out to visit Grandmother often. In the spring they helped her plant a vegetable garden and flowers. Mary Jo played with the baby chicks and fed the hens.

125

In the summer Mary Jo and her brother Jeff waded in the creek. They picked blackberries.

Mary Jo's father always told Grandmother, "You still make the best berry pie in the world."

And Mary Jo's grandmother always laughed and said, "You just say that because it's true."

But after the leaves began to fall from the trees and the days grew colder, Mary Jo's mother and father began to worry.

"You haven't even got a telephone. You shouldn't be living all alone way out here," said Mary Jo's mother. "Why, your nearest neighbor is out beyond the main road."

Grandmother smiled. "Now don't you worry about me. I'm as snug as can be here. Don't you fret about me."

To be *snug* is to be cozy or comfortable.

Every year the family had Christmas dinner at Grandmother's. This year, for the first time, Mary Jo was staying on at Grandmother's by herself. After dinner she and Grandmother waved good-bye to everybody from the porch. It was very quiet. Grandmother looked out over the bare trees at the sky. "Snow tonight," she said.

Just before she fell asleep, Mary Jo saw great flakes of snow, like feathers, falling outside the window.

Even though Mary Jo woke early next morning, she could already hear Grandmother in the kitchen.

"Beautiful snow, beautiful snow," sang Mary Jo when she looked out the window.

"This is the most snow I ever saw here this early in the winter," said Grandmother, putting biscuits into the oven. "Here, Mary Jo, take these bread crumbs out to the birds. I'm going to get some jam from the back pantry."

Mary Jo had to sweep the snow ahead of herself so she could walk out on the porch. She swept one corner of the porch. Then she put out the crumbs. Before she was back inside the door, hungry birds were there to eat.

Grandmother had not come back from the pantry yet. From the open pantry door, Mary Jo heard a moan. Grandmother called, "Mary Jo!"

"What happened?" said Mary Jo running to the door. She looked down. Her grandmother was lying on the pantry floor. She had fallen down the steps.

"I can't get up," moaned Grandmother.

"I'm coming! I'll help you," said Mary Jo.

"Take the biscuits out of the oven first," said Grandmother.

Mary Jo hurried to the oven, opened the door, and lifted the biscuits out. Then she hurried to the pantry. But when Mary Jo knelt beside her grandmother and tried to lift her, Grandmother cried out with pain.

"No, Mary Jo, don't try to lift me. My leg hurts too much to move it," she said. "Now I'm in a fine fix!"

"Don't worry, Grandmother," said Mary Jo. She ran into the bedroom and got blankets to wrap around her grandmother. She carefully put a pillow under her head.

"Thank goodness you are here, Mary Jo," Grandmother said. "Just let me rest while I think of what to do. I'll be all right. You go and have some breakfast while the biscuits are hot."

Mary Jo poured some coffee for her
grandmother. Then, while she ate a biscuit,
she looked out the window at the falling
snow. I don't even have my boots here, she
thought.

Mary Jo knew that she must go for help. On a day like this, no one would be passing by on the little road where her grandmother lived. She would have to walk to the main road.

"I'm going up to the main road for help," said Mary Jo.

"In all this snow?" said Grandmother.

"I can do it," said Mary Jo.

Grandmother sighed. "I guess I'll have to let you go, Mary Jo," she said. "Wrap up good and warm."

"Yes, Grandmother," said Mary Jo. "You rest and don't worry."

"I'll be all right. I'm a tough old bird," said Grandmother. Then she leaned her head back and closed her eyes.

Mary Jo found a pair of boots in a closet. She made them fit by stuffing the toes full of newspaper. She put on two sweaters, a coat, and an old stocking cap. Then she hurried out into the snow.

The snow had stopped falling, but icy wind blew into her face. Mary Jo walked as fast as she could down the long drive.

It took her twice as long as it usually did just to reach the old mailbox. The snow in the road was untouched. No truck or car had been along.

Mary Jo walked on toward the main road, lifting her feet high at each step in the old heavy boots. She had never felt so much alone.

When she finally reached the main
highway, Mary Jo could see that no cars
had been along there, either. The snow was
too deep. Mary Jo's legs had never felt so
tired.

Then up the road she saw a black speck
moving slowly closer. She stared at it.
Then she waved. "It's the snowplow!" she
cried out loud.

A *snowplow* is a vehi-
cle used to push snow
off a road.

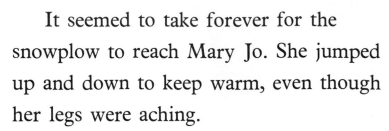

It seemed to take forever for the snowplow to reach Mary Jo. She jumped up and down to keep warm, even though her legs were aching.

The driver stopped and leaned over. "What are you doing out here, little girl?"

Mary Jo explained to him what had happened. "Can you call my father in town? His name is William Wood."

"Sure!" said the man. "Here, climb up. We'll clear the road down to your grandmother's house. We'll let you off there. Then I'll go on to the next house and phone your father."

When Mary Jo got off at her grandmother's drive, she waved good-bye and walked back up to the house.

Grandmother's eyes were open and she smiled. "How did you get back so fast, child?"

Mary Jo told her about the snowplow. "Mother and Dad will be here in a little while," she said. "All our worries are over now, Grandmother. I'll go heat some soup."

"That sounds good," said Grandmother. "I'm feeling better already. Thank goodness you were here, Mary Jo."

Discussion Question *When have you been able to help someone?*
Enriching Activities **1.** *Safety discussion.* Discuss what the children could do if they needed help; for example, if they were locked out of their houses, if there was a fire, or if someone was injured. Ask the children to list people they could call in an emergency, such as relatives, police and fire departments, neighbors, and hospitals. You may want to discuss the emergency telephone numbers in your local telephone directory and encourage the children to learn their parents' day phone numbers. **2.** *Related reading.* Some children may want to read the other Mary Jo books by Janice May Udry. See page T61 for the titles of these books.

Questions

1. How did Mary Jo show she was brave?

   1. Literal / recall
   She went to get help by herself. (pages 134–138)

2. How did Grandmother show she was brave?

   2. Literal / recall
   She stayed alone while Mary Jo went for help. (pages 134–140)

3. Grandmother's family was unhappy that she lived alone, but Grandmother said, "Don't you *fret* about me." What did she mean?

   3. Vocabulary and Interpretive / inference "Don't worry"; "Don't get upset." (page 127)

4. What do you think happened after the story ended?

   4. Interpretive / extrapolation Possible answers: Mary Jo's parents arrived; Grandmother continued to live in the country.

Activity

Interpretive / extrapolation *Writing lists.* Possible answers: get a telephone; have someone check in on Grandmother every day; have a friend come to live with her.

Mary Jo's grandmother still wants to live in the country. Mary Jo is making a list of things that Grandmother can do to be safe in the country. Add three more things to Mary Jo's list.

To Be Safe
1. Put a light in the pantry.
2.
3.
4.

Words to Know
drift: to move or float along in air or water.
melting: changing from a solid to a liquid, usually by heat.

Introducing the Poem *In this very short poem, Kazue Mizumura says that she can "taste" winter. As we read the poem, try to understand what "tasting winter" means.*

Snowflakes drift.
I taste winter
melting on my lips.

A poem by Kazue Mizumura
Pronounced /kä·zōō·ā′   mē·zōō′·mû·rä/.

Discussion Questions *What word could we use instead of* winter *in the poem?* (Snowflakes.) *How could you "taste" summer?* (Possible answer: by drinking lemonade.) *How could you "taste" spring?* (Possible answer: by catching raindrops in my mouth.)
Enriching Activities **1.** *Writing verses.* Have the children choose a season and list three or four words associated with it. *Snowman, gray,* and *cold,* for example, might be associated with winter. Then have the children follow the pattern of the poem in writing their own short verses about a season, such as *Sand blows./I feel summer/touching my face; Leaves crunch./I hear fall/beneath my feet.* **2.** *Snowflake mobiles.* Have each child cut several snowflakes from folded sheets of white paper. Help them tie long strings to the snowflakes and hang them from wire coat hangers.

Picture by Stan Tusan

143

Soft Grass

A poem

Objectives ● To recognize the use of contrast in a poem. ● To relate the main idea (theme) of a poem to personal experience.
Introducing the Poem *What can you do in soft grass? (Possible answer: have a picnic.) What can you do on a sidewalk? (Possible answer: ride a bike.) This poem tells how someone feels about the grass and the sidewalk. See if you feel the same way.*

The sidewalk is hard
Beneath my feet.
Hard, hot sidewalk,
Hard, hot street.

Stony sidewalk,
Stony yard,
Stony buildings,
Hot and hard.

But I go to the park
Along my street,
Where the grass is soft
Beneath my feet.

144

Picture by Carol Newsom

Off of the sidewalk,
Out of the sun,
Over the cool, soft grass
I run!

Rope Rhyme

A poem by Eloise Greenfield

Get set, ready now, jump right in
Bounce and kick and giggle and spin
Listen to the rope when it hits the ground
Listen to that clappedy-slappedy sound
Jump right up when it tells you to
Come back down, whatever you do
Count to a hundred, count by ten
Start to count all over again
That's what jumping is all about
Get set, ready now, jump right out!

Picture by Sharon Harker

BOOKSHELF

"I Can't," Said the Ant by Polly Cameron. Coward, McCann & Geoghegan, 1961. Miss Teapot falls and breaks her spout. An army of ants and spiders come to help her. This story is told in rhyme. **Reading Level** Easy

Rafiki by Nola Langner. Viking Press, 1977. Rafiki wants to build her own house. Some animals want her to clean their house instead. Will Rafiki have to do what the animals say? **Reading Level** Average

I Can Do It Myself by Lessie Jones Little and Eloise Greenfield. T. Y. Crowell, 1978. Donny wants to buy his mother a birthday present. He goes to the store with his wagon all by himself, but a big bulldog gets in his way going home. **Reading Level** Average

Sumi's Prize by Yoshiko Uchida. Charles Scribner's Sons, 1964. Sumi wants to win the kite-flying contest, but the wind makes a problem that only Sumi can fix. **Reading Level** Average

148

Animals
All Around

Can You Guess?

Riddles in rhyme by Beatrice Schenk de Regniers

Objectives ● To use word, picture, and rhyme clues to solve riddles. ● To write riddles.

Introducing the Riddles *The animals in this picture are enjoying a picnic. Some of them are described in these riddles. As you read the riddles, see if you can guess the answers.*

It has two feet,

No hands, two wings.

It can fly

In the sky.

Sometimes it chirps.

Sometimes it sings

The sweetest song

You ever heard.

Can you guess?

It is a . . .

bird.

Six legs for walking.

Mouth for eating—not talking.

Does not make a sound.

Sleeps under the ground.

Likes picnics, but can't

Bring its own. It's an . . .

ant.

A short short tail.
A long long nose
It uses for
A water hose.

Two great big ears.
Four great big feet.
A tiny peanut
Is a treat.

Its name is El—
Oh, no! I can't!
Now *you* tell *me:*
An . . .

elephant.

Picture by Ron LeHew

151

Caballito

A Mexican rhyme

Objectives ● To enjoy a poem written in two languages. ● To recognize that repetition creates rhythm in a poem.

Introducing the Poem *This poem is written in two languages, Spanish and English. It is about a boy riding a pony. As I read it, see if the words make you feel as if you are riding.* Read the poem at a steady, rhythmical pace.

Word to Know
   galloping: going at a fast pace.

Discussion Questions *How do you think Antonio feels while he is riding?* (Possible answers: scared; excited; proud.) *What words tell you that Antonio is enjoying his ride?* ("Watch us go!"; "Long live Antonio!")

Caballito, caballito,

kä·bä·yē′·tō   kä·bä·yē′·tō

No me tumbes, no me tumbes;

nō mä tōōm′·bäs nō mä tōōm′·bäs

a galope y a galope

ä gä·lō′·pā ē ä gä·lō′·pā

recio, recio, recio.

rā′·sē·ō rā′·sē·ō rā′·sē·ō

¡Qué viva Antonio!

kā bē′·bä än·tō′·nē·ō

Little pony, little pony,

Do not throw me, do not throw me;

Galloping, galloping,

Watch us go!

Long live Antonio!

Enriching Activity *Rhythm chorus.* Divide the children into two groups. Have one group read the first half of the three lines beginning the poem, and the fourth line. Have the other group read the second half of the poem's first three lines, and the last line. Then tell the children to read the poem again, this time at a faster pace to show the poem's galloping rhythm. Repeat the activity for the Spanish version.

Picture by Raphael & Bolognese

153

Objectives ● To identify different points of view. ● To learn about animal care. ● To extend a story by writing a sequel.

Synopsis of the Story Rrra-ah, a toad very content in his own surroundings, is captured by three children who want him for a pet. Rrra-ah's efforts to escape cause such catastrophes in the house that Mother insists that the children return him to the meadow. The children take Rrra-ah back, and he resumes his peaceful life.

Reading Level Average

Rrra-ah

From a story by Eros Keith

Pictures by Terrence Meagher

Rrra-ah was in his favorite place, on top of a big white clover. He could see everything, the trees and flowers, and the pond where he was born. As he lifted his head, he could feel the summer breeze.

Rrra-ah stuck his nose into a pink clover. He closed his eyes and took a deep breath.

Introducing the Story *How do you feel when you are enjoying yourself and someone bothers you? Rrra-ah is a story about a toad who lives very happily in a meadow—that is, until some children come along and bother him. As we read this story, think about how you would feel if you were Rrra-ah.*

Words to Know
  clover: a plant with leaves usually having three leaflets but sometimes four. (page 154)
  escape: to get free. (page 160)
  crashed: made a loud noise. (page 161)

155

He opened his eyes. It was dark!
The sun has fallen, he thought. Then
he heard voices calling, "Look over
here! I've got one!" And Rrra-ah
knew what had happened.

The sun hadn't fallen. He had been
caught!

Rrra-ah saw three children. *Boak! How big and ugly they are!* he thought.

"Ugh! Is he ugly!" said one of the girls. "I think he's cute," said the boy. "He's just a baby," the other girl said.

It was a long way from Rrra-ah's meadow to the children's house. He had been dumped into a big glass jar. Rrra-ah sat very still and watched his pond get smaller and smaller.

A *meadow* (line 8) is an area of grassland.

157

"Do you think Mother will let you keep him?"

I hope not! thought Rrra-ah.

"What are you going to call him?"

Rrra-ah called his name as loud as he could.

"Frog—just Frog," said the girl with the jar.

Frog! I'm not a frog! thought Rrra-ah. *I'm a toad and my name is Rrra-ah.*

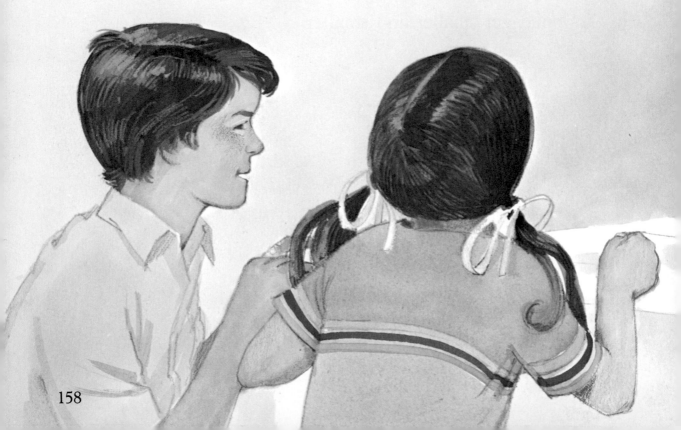

"Mother, look! We found a frog!"

Rrra-ah! Rrra-ah! croaked Rrra-ah.

"Well, you didn't find him in the bathtub," said Mother. "You'll have to find another place to keep him."

Oh, no! thought Rrra-ah. *They are going to keep me!*

One girl brought a box. One girl brought some grass. And the boy brought Rrra-ah turtle food.

Rrra-ah didn't like the box or the turtle food. He didn't eat. He didn't sleep. *I'm not a frog,* he kept thinking. *And I'm not a turtle either!*

In the morning one girl said, "Frog, are you ready to play games with us?"

I'm ready to play escape, thought Rrra-ah, and he leaped from the girl's hands.

He crashed through the living room,
the dining room, the hall. And he
tipped over three lamps and a vase
full of flowers. But he didn't escape.
The children caught him.

That night Rrra-ah was very hungry
and sad. He heard moths at the window
and crickets in the grass. But he couldn't
hear the toads by his pond. It was too
far away. He didn't sleep because
he was thinking about escaping.

The next day Rrra-ah played the escape
game again.

"Stop him!" cried Mother. "He's
headed for the kitchen!"

SPLAT!

"That does it!" said Mother. "That frog has got to go!"

At last! thought Rrra-ah.

The children carried Rrra-ah back to his meadow. "This is good-bye, Frog," one girl said. "We'll miss your games," said the other. "Maybe we'll see you next summer," said the boy.

Oh, no you won't! thought Rrra-ah. And he was gone.

Then he could see it! His favorite place! He jumped up and there were the trees and the flowers, and the pond where he was born. Rrra-ah stuck his nose into his pink clover, closed his eyes and took a deep breath.

The sun went down behind the trees and from the pond he heard other voices calling, *Rrra-ah. Rrra-ah.*

Discussion Questions *What voices were calling Rrra-ah at the end of the story?* (Other toads.) *Why was Rrra-ah happier in the meadow than at the children's home?* (Possible answers: he liked the pond and the clover in the meadow; he did not like his box or the turtle food in the children's home.)

Enriching Activities **1.** *Making books/research.* Divide the class into groups. Have each group choose an animal and research its care. Then have the children draw illustrations and write sentences describing each aspect of the animal's care. Put the groups' work together to form a class animal-care book. **2.** *Story extension.* Have the children write stories about an adventure that Rrra-ah had after he got home.

Questions

1. Why did Rrra-ah think the sun had fallen?

2. What do you think *boak* means in "toad talk"?

3. What food wouldn't Rrra-ah eat?

4. What was Rrra-ah's favorite game?

5. Why was Rrra-ah happy at the end of the story?

1. Literal/recall He was in the dark when he was caught. (page 156)
2. Interpretive/inference Possible answer: "Ugh." (page 157)
3. Literal/recall Turtle food. (page 160)
4. Interpretive/inference Escape. (page 160)
5. Interpretive/inference He was home again. (page 164)

Activity

Boak is a "toad word." Make a list of three other "toad words." Then make a list of three words another animal might say. Give each list a title. Write or draw what each word means.

Vocabulary *Writing/drawing.* Encourage the children to list unusual animal sounds, such as "hrut" for a toad, as well as conventional animal sounds, such as "oink."

You Can't Make a Turtle Come Out

From a song by Malvina Reynolds

Objectives ● To note repetition in a song.
● To show similarities and differences within a category.

Introducing the Song *Why might a turtle hide in its shell?* (To sleep; to hide from danger.) *Here are the words to a song about a turtle and its shell.*

Discussion Question *What does "You can knock on the door" mean in the song?* (You can knock on the turtle's shell.)

Enriching Activities **1.** *Animal art.* Ask the children to name other animals with shells, such as snails, clams, and crabs. Then have them choose an animal and make a model of it. They might make turtles with egg cartons and construction paper (a neck can be made with an accordion-folded strip of paper); snails with clay; clams with folded paper plates; and crabs with paper and paper fasteners (to make moveable legs). Encourage the children to decorate their animals in realistic or fanciful ways. **2.** *Singing.* Teach the children the song's melody and the rest of its verses. (See page T59.)

You can't make a turtle come out,

You can't make a turtle come out,

You can coax him or call him or shake

    him or shout,

To *coax* is to ask for something in a gentle or flattering way.

But you can't make a turtle come out,

    come out,

You can't make a turtle come out.

If he wants to stay in his shell,

If he wants to stay in his shell,

You can knock on the door but you

    can't ring the bell,

And you can't make a turtle come out,

    come out,

You can't make a turtle come out.

Picture by Fran Stiles

167

Three Little Animals

Poems by Ernesto Galarza

Objectives ● To enjoy poems written in two languages. ● To recognize that poems may have factual content.

Introducing the Poems *A caterpillar grows up to be a butterfly or a moth. This is a scientific fact. These next poems tell interesting facts about three other little animals. The poems are in Spanish and English.*

A ciencia cierta
ä·sē·en′·sē·ä sē̄·er′·tä
el renacuajo
el rä·nä·kwä′·hō
será mañana
sä·rä′ mä·nyä′·nä
una rana.
o͞o′·nä rä′·nä

It's a scientific fact
that a frog
is a grown-up
pollywog.

Lombriz soterrada
lōm·brēs′ sō·te·rä′·thä

trabaja, trabaja
trä·bä′·hä trä·bä′·hä

callada, callada.
kä·yä′·thä kä·yä′·thä

An earthworm doesn't make a sound when he's working underground.

Pictures by Pat Welch and Michael Dowdall

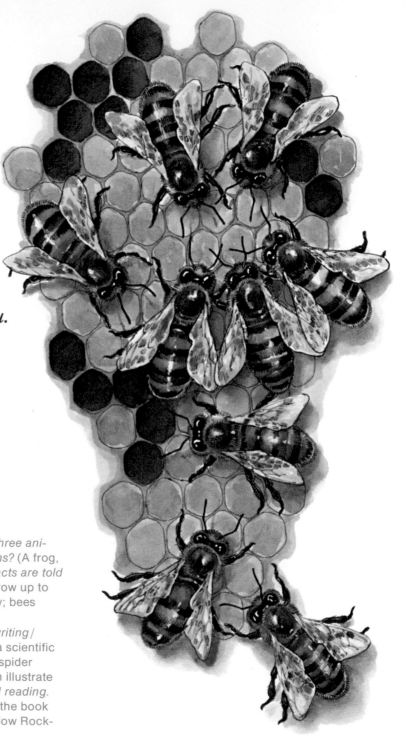

Una vez era
ōō′·nä bās ä′·rä
una abeja mielera
ōō′·nä ä·bä′·hä mē·āy·lä′·rä
en panal de cera.
en pä·näl′ dā sä′·rä

Bees won't bother you.

Relax.

They are busy

making wax.

Discussion Questions   *What three animals are talked about in the poems?* (A frog, an earthworm, and bees.) *What facts are told about each animal?* (Pollywogs grow up to be frogs; earthworms work quietly; bees make wax.)

Enriching Activities   1. *Fact writing/ drawing.* Have the children write a scientific fact about an animal, such as ''A spider catches flies for food.'' Have them illustrate the facts in drawings.   **2.** *Related reading.* The children might enjoy reading the book *Olly's Pollywogs* by Anne and Harlow Rockwell (Doubleday, 1970).

About ERNESTO GALARZA

Did you ever watch a bee walk across the face of a flower? Did you ever listen to waves booming on the shore? As a boy in Mexico, Ernesto Galarza spent many hours watching and listening to nature.

He says, "We had no radio or television or movies. We had Nature. . . . We learned to use all our senses to hear, feel, smell, and taste all of Nature's performance around us. . . . We put all this together in ways that pleased our fancy. We were poets. Many, many years after I had left my village I tried to remember how we made poetry. And I still try."

More Books by Ernesto Galarza

Spiders in the House   (University of Notre Dame Press, 1970)

Poemas Pe-que Pe-que Pe-que-nitos (Little Poems)   (Editorial Almadén Library, 1972)

Rimas Tontas (Nutty Rhymes)   (Editorial Almadén Library, 1971)

Zoo-Risa (Fun at the Zoo)   (Editorial Almadén Library, 1971)

Animals in the Library

Storybooks: *Mouse Soup; Winnie-the-Pooh; Oscar Otter; How Hippo!* Fact books: *Elephants of Africa; Baby Farm Animals; Birds at Night; Let's Get Turtles.*

Make a list of the four books Fred will choose. Write *Storybooks* at the top of the list. Make a list of the four books Sue will choose. Write *Fact Books* at the top.

Pictures by Ed Taber

Storybooks

- Frances Ant's Trip
- Fishy Gets Caught
- Dinah the Dinosaur
- The Three Little Pigs

Fact Books

- Dinosaur World
- Fish as Pets
- Caring for Small Pets
- All About Wolves

Answers: 1. *Dinosaur World.*
2. *Caring for Small Pets.*
3. *Fishy Gets Caught.*
4. *All About Wolves.*

Choose a book for each animal.

1 I like dinosaurs. Where can I find out more about them?

2 I have a new pet ant. What can I feed her?

3 My goldfish wants to hear a fish story. What can I read to him?

4 I want to find out what wolves like to eat.

Dinosaur Time

Reading Level Average

From the story by Peggy Parish

Pictures by Phyllis Rockne

Objectives ● To show similarities and differences within a category. ● To use point of view to explore nonfiction.

Long, long ago
the world was different.
More land was under water.
It was warm all the time.
And dinosaurs were everywhere. . . .

174

There were big dinosaurs.
There were small ones.
There were fast dinosaurs
and slow ones.
Some dinosaurs ate meat.
Some ate plants.

This dinosaur was a giant.
But its mouth was tiny.
It ate plants.
It ate, and ate, and ate
to fill up its big body.
Its name is Brontosaurus
(BRON·tuh·SAWR·us).

This dinosaur was small.
It was as big as a cat.
But it could run fast.
It could catch other animals
and eat them.
Its name is Compsognathus
(comp·SOG·nuh·thus).

This dinosaur was fat.
It was too fat to run from enemies.
That is why it stayed in the water.
It was safe there,
and food was close by.
It ate plants.
Its name is Brachiosaurus
(BRAK·ee·oh·SAWR·us).

This dinosaur was a plant-eater.
It had five horns.
Its name is Pentaceratops
(PEN•tuh•SEHR•uh•tops).
This name is just right.
It means "five-horns-on-the-face."

This dinosaur
was the biggest meat-eater.
Its jaws were huge.
Its teeth were six inches long.
It ate other dinosaurs.
Its name is Tyrannosaurus
(tih·RAN·uh·SAWR·us).

Dinosaurs lived everywhere
for a long time.
Then they died.
Nobody knows why.
But once it was their world.
It was dinosaur time.

Author's Note

We do not know much about
dinosaurs. No one ever saw a dinosaur.

But people have found dinosaur
fossils, such as footprints, bones, and
teeth. Scientists study them, and can tell
how big the dinosaurs were, what they
ate, and other things about the way they
lived.

Scientists learn more each year. But
we may never know all about dinosaurs.

Questions

1. Who will win a race?

   Brachiosaurus   Compsognathus

2. Who will hide in the water?

   Brontosaurus   Brachiosaurus

3. Who will eat a flower?

   Brontosaurus   Tyrannosaurus

4. Who has a name with "five" in it?

   Compsognathus   Pentaceratops

Activity

Be a dinosaur. Answer Cynthia's letter. Tell which dinosaur you are.

Dear Dinosaur,
Why aren't you living today? Please tell me what you would do if you were alive now.
Your friend,
Cynthia

"How" and "Why" Stories

People have always wondered about the world. They have wondered how the elephant got its trunk. They have wondered why the sun and the moon are in the sky. Long ago, people made up stories to explain these things. These "how" and "why" stories came from many lands. This one is from West Africa.

How Spider Got a Bald Head

Objectives ● To recognize a *pourquoi* (explanatory) tale. ● To interpret a pourquoi tale through puppetry.

Introducing the Lesson *Can you tell me how zebras got their stripes, or why there are stars in the sky? People used to make up stories to answer such "how and why" questions. Usually the stories told why people and animals look and act the way they do. Some stories told about happenings in nature, such as thunder or earthquakes. Sometimes the stories were very funny. In this story, we will read how the spider lost its hair.*

Pictures by Ed Taber

183

Discussion Questions *Why was Spider doing the Hat-Shaking Dance?* (The beans on his head were hot.) *What made Spider bald?* (The beans burned his hair off.)
Enriching Activities **1.** *Puppetry.* Divide the children into three groups to present a class pourquoi tale. Have the first group write the pourquoi tale using one of the suggested titles on page 184, or have them choose one of the stories they have already written. Help the second group make paper-bag puppets or flannelboard figures of the characters. Have the children in the third group use the puppets to perform the tale for the class. **2.** *Science.* Invite a veterinarian or a zoologist to speak to the class about interesting and unusual animal traits and behavior.

Before the children write their own stories, read them some other pourquoi tales. See page T62 for titles of pourquoi tales from several countries.

Write or draw your own "how" or "why" story. Tell why an animal looks a certain way, or tell why something happens in nature. Choose one of these story titles, or make up your own title.

Why the Turtle Hides in Its Shell
How Frogs Lost Their Tails
Why There Is Thunder and Lightning

BOOKSHELF

How Puppies Grow by Millicent E. Selsam.
Four Winds Press, 1971. Six little puppies
are growing up day by day, week by week.
What they eat, what they do, and what
they learn is shown in photographs.   **Reading Level** Easy

Millions of Cats by Wanda Gág.
Coward-McCann, 1928. An old woman
and an old man want one cat to care for.
What will they do with the millions of cats
that show up at their door?   **Reading Level** Easy

Sky Dog by Brinton Turkle. Viking Press, 1969.
A boy imagines he sees a cloud take the
shape of a dog. He wishes he could have
the sky dog. Then the boy finds a real dog.
Will he be able to keep him?   **Reading Level** Average

Ji-Nongo-Nongo Means Riddles by Verna
Aardema. Four Winds Press, 1978. These
riddles come from many places in Africa.
Some of the riddles are about animals.
Others are about the jobs people have.   **Reading Level** Challenging

186

5 Long, Long Ago

Heart of the Woods

A poem by Wesley Curtright

Objectives ● To recognize the feeling (mood) of a poem. ● To respond to a poem through another medium.

Deep into the woods we'll go,
Hand in hand.
Let the woods close about us,
Let the world outside be lost—
And let us find that Secret City
Lost so long ago—
In the Heart of the Woods.

Introducing the Poem *These stories and poems are about mysterious, unknown, and magical things. In the first poem we'll search for a secret place. Let's find out what is deep in the heart of the woods.*

Discussion Questions *What is in the heart of the woods?* (A secret city.) *Why do you think it is a secret city?* (Possible answers: there are hidden treasures in the city; the people don't want to be found.)

Enriching Activities 1. *Model construction.* Discuss what the Secret City might look like, asking if it is a walled city, a fort, or a castle. Then help the class to plan and construct a model of its own Secret City. Provide boxes, corrugated paper, mailing tubes, aluminum foil, coffee cans, plastic wrap, glue, and paint for the construction. **2.** *Extending experiences.* Have the children describe places that seem magical or secret.

Picture by Christa Kieffer

Reading Level Challenging

The Magic Porridge Pot

A German folk tale retold by Paul Galdone

Pictures by Jane Teiko Oka

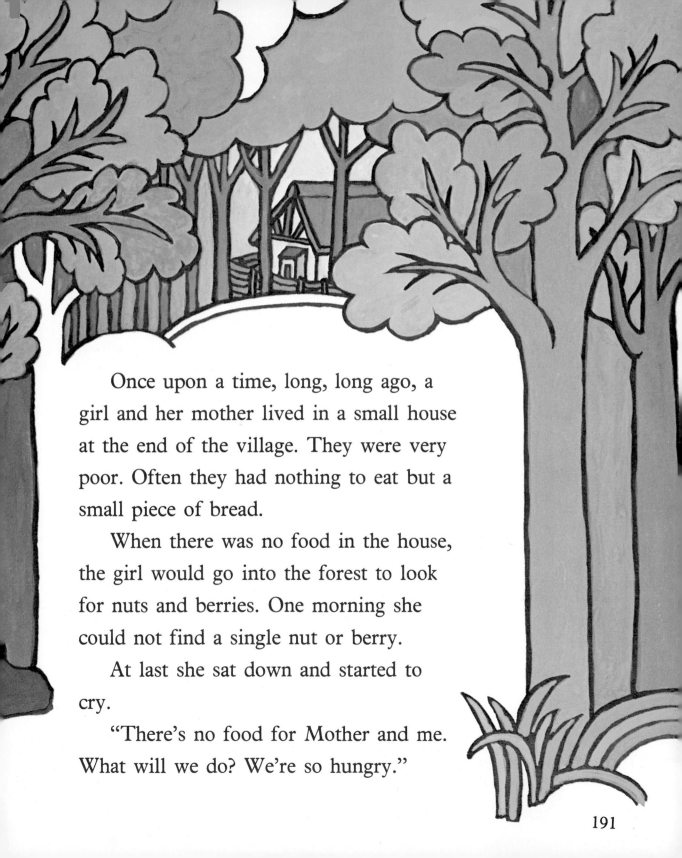

Once upon a time, long, long ago, a girl and her mother lived in a small house at the end of the village. They were very poor. Often they had nothing to eat but a small piece of bread.

When there was no food in the house, the girl would go into the forest to look for nuts and berries. One morning she could not find a single nut or berry.

At last she sat down and started to cry.

"There's no food for Mother and me. What will we do? We're so hungry."

"Cheer up, my dear," said a friendly voice.

The girl looked up in surprise. She saw a woman who wore a long <u>cloak</u> and leaned on a crooked stick.

"Do not worry, my dear," said the woman. "You will never be hungry again."

A *cloak* is a kind of coat, usually without sleeves.

192

From under her cloak she took out a small black pot.

"This is a magic pot, my dear. Put it on the fire. Say to it,

'Boil, Little Pot, boil!'

and at once it will fill up with delicious porridge. When you have had all you can eat, say to it,

'Stop, Little Pot, stop!'

Then the magic pot will stop boiling."

"Oh, thank you so much," said the girl.

"Never forget the magic words, my dear," said the woman. "Never forget!" And no sooner had she said this than she disappeared.

The girl carried the pot home as fast as she could run.

"What have you got?" her mother asked when she saw the pot.

"This is a magic pot that will cook delicious porridge," the girl answered. "A woman in the forest gave it to me."

The girl was eager to try out the magic pot. She set it on the fire and said,

"Boil, Little Pot, boil!"

Sure enough, delicious porridge bubbled up.

When they had had all that they could eat, the girl said,

"Stop, Little Pot, stop!"

and the magic pot stopped boiling.

For a long time the girl and her mother had as much porridge as they wanted. They were very happy.

Then one day the girl went to visit her friend at the other end of the village. She was gone a long while and her mother began to be hungry. So she set the magic pot on the fire and said to it,

"Boil, Little Pot, boil!"

The porridge began to fill the pot, and the mother dished out a nice bowlful.

Soon the porridge was bubbling at the top of the pot. But the mother had forgotten the magic words. The porridge kept on coming. It began to spill over the top.

"Halt, Little Pot, halt!" the mother said.

The porridge only boiled and bubbled over faster.

"Enough, Little Pot, enough!" cried the mother, trying to remember the right words.

The porridge went right on bubbling over. Soon it covered the floor of the cottage.

The mother struggled to the door and opened it wide to let the porridge out of the house.

"No more, Little Pot, no more!" she shouted.

The stream of porridge ran through the cottage door and onto the street. Down the street ran the mother crying, **"Cease, Little Pot, cease!"** But the porridge went on and on, toward the very last house in the village where the girl was visiting.

When the mother came to the house she called, "Help, help! The magic pot keeps boiling, boiling, boiling!"

At once the girl guessed what was wrong. So she waded into the thick, heavy porridge and ran home as fast as she could, with her mother behind her.

When the girl reached the cottage she cried,

> "Stop, Little Pot, stop!
> Stop, Little Pot, stop!
> Stop, Little Pot, stop!
> Stop, Little Pot, stop!"

And the magic pot stopped boiling.

Then everyone in the village came out
into the street carrying dippers, spoons,
cups, bowls, and buckets. They dipped up
the porridge, and they scooped up the
porridge, and they spooned up the porridge.
There was enough porridge for everyone to
eat for days and days.

After that, the girl and her mother
and the people of the village never went
hungry. And they never forgot the words
to stop the magic pot from boiling.

Discussion Questions Have the class turn back to page 190. *Look under the story title. This folk tale is retold by Paul Galdone. What do you think it means to retell a story?* (The writer did not make up the story.) *What were the magical things in the folk tale?* (The porridge pot; the woman who gave the pot to the girl; the magical commands.)

Enriching Activity *Making bookmarks.* Ask the children to think of other magical objects used in stories. A few examples are Aladdin's lamp, the queen's mirror in *Snow White,* and the cakes and potion that made Alice grow and shrink in Wonderland. Supply the children with construction paper to make bookmarks labeled "My Magical Bookmark." Have them decorate the bookmarks with cutouts, paintings, and drawings of magical objects.

Questions

1. What did the mother forget?

2. Why did the girl say, "Stop, Little Pot, stop!" four times instead of just once?

3. Which word best tells about the pot?

     silly   magic   black

4. Which word does *not* tell what the pot did?

          boiled   bubbled   cried

1. Literal/recall She forgot the magic words that stopped the pot. (page 196)
2. Interpretive/ inference Possible answer: because the pot had been boiling so long, more magical power was needed. (page 199)
3. Vocabulary Magic. (page 193)
4. Interpretive/ inference Cried.

Activity **Interpretive/extrapolation** *Writing/drawing.*

Here is a magic box. Write the magic words that make the box work. Draw what happens when you say them.

201

Some One

A poem by Walter de la Mare

Objectives ● To recognize that repetition and rhyme affect the feeling (mood) of a poem. ● To identify a character's point of view.

Introducing the Poem *Sometimes we hear strange noises, and when we look to see what made them, nothing is there! Let's see what happens when the elf in this poem hears a knock on his door.*
Discussion Questions *What was knocking on the door? (The poem doesn't tell us.) What repeating words make the poem seem mysterious? (Sure; at all.) What other words give the poem a mysterious feeling? (Possible answers: still dark night; tap-tapping; knocking.)*
Enriching Activity *Letter writing.* Have the children pretend to be the elf in the poem and write a letter to another elf friend telling about the strange knocking. Ask the children to write a surprise ending that tells who knocked. Point out that the explanation should be consistent with the small size of the elf and other creatures in the poem.

Some one came knocking
    At my wee, small door;
Some one came knocking,
    I'm sure—sure—sure;
I listened, I opened,
    I looked to left and right,
But nought there was a-stirring
    In the still dark night;
Only the busy beetle
    Tap-tapping in the wall,
Only from the forest
    The screech-owl's call,
Only the cricket whistling
    While the dewdrops fall,
So I know not who came knocking,
    At all, at all, at all.

If something is *a-stirring,* it is moving about.

202

Picture by Judith Gwyn Brown

Objectives ● To identify the tone of a folk tale. ● To infer a character's point of view by extending the story. ● To recognize fantasy in stories.

Synopsis of the Folk Tale A hunter and his tame bear take shelter in the home of a farmer and his family. That night some trolls invade the house. When a troll begins to tease the bear, the bear throws him out the door. The other trolls hastily retreat, never to bother Farmer Neils again.

Reading Level Average

The Trolls and the Pussy Cat

Adapted from the Norwegian folk tale retold by George Jonsen

Pictures by Kinuko Craft

Introducing the Folk Tale   *Strange things happen every night at Farmer Neils's house. As we read, think of what you might do in the same situation.*

Words to Know
tame: naturally wild but made gentle and unafraid of humans. (page 205)
trolls: in folklore, mischievous dwarfs or giants that live underground or in caves. (page 206)

There was once a hunter who lived in the far north. One day he caught a big white bear. He had never seen a bear so big and so white and so tame. I will take this bear to the king, he thought.

But soon the snow began to fall. The wind began to blow. The hunter was very cold. He stopped at a small house and knocked at the door.

The door opened right away. There stood a farmer and his family all dressed in heavy coats and boots.

"May I stay the night with you?" asked the hunter. "The snow and ice have frozen my poor bear and me."

"Ah! You would not want to stay in
this house," said the farmer. "The trolls
will be coming down the mountain tonight.
They eat our food. They sleep in our
beds. We are lucky if they don't break
all our dishes and tables and chairs."

"We are going to leave," said the
farmer's wife. "We are going to sleep in
a cave in the woods."

"Wait!" said the hunter. "Don't go.
Let my bear and me stay here with you.
Maybe we can help you."

So the bear crawled under the table. The hunter lay down on the floor with a blanket. And the farmer's family went to sleep in their own beds.

They did not sleep for long. Soon there was a loud noise outside the door.

"Farmer Neils! Farmer Neils! We have come for our dinner. Open the door and let us in."

The door flew open and in ran the
trolls. They ran into the kitchen. They
pulled out the dishes. They carried out
great bowls of food and began eating it.

Suddenly a little troll looked under
the table. He saw the bear's white nose.
"Look here!" he called. "I see a pussy
cat! Nice pussy cat!"

He put some hot meat on a long stick.
He poked it at the bear's nose.

With a roar, the bear jumped out, picked up the troll, and threw him right out the door.

You never saw such a thing! Trolls were running out the door. Trolls were jumping out the windows. One even climbed up the chimney!

The next morning the hunter and his bear set off to see the king. Before long everyone had heard about Farmer Neils and his big pussy cat. And from that day on no more trolls came to visit his house.

Discussion Question *What would you have done if the trolls had invaded your house?* (Encourage imaginative answers, such as hiding the food and the dishes.)
Enriching Activities **1.** *Story Theater.* Have the children act out the story using the Story Theater techniques in the front of this book. Encourage the children to emphasize the humor at the end of the tale, when the trolls scramble about looking for exits.
2. *Reading table.* Have the children collect stories and folk tales about imaginary creatures such as trolls, elves, and giants. A few suggestions are Paul Galdone's *The Three Billy Goats Gruff* (Seabury, 1973); *The Elves and the Shoemaker* by the Brothers Grimm (Four Winds Press, 1975); and *Molly and the Giant* by Kurt Werth (Parents' Magazine Press, 1973).

Questions

1. What were Farmer Neils and his family afraid of?
2. Where was the hunter taking the bear?
3. Which word tells the most about this story?

   scary funny true

4. The hunter was not afraid of the bear because the bear was

   big cold tame

1. Literal/recall Trolls. (page 206)
2. Literal/recall To the king. (page 205)
3. Interpretive/inference Funny.
4. Vocabulary Tame. (page 205)

Activity

Interpretive/extrapolation *Story extension.*

Be one of the trolls who visited Farmer Neils's house. Write what happened to you. What did you say and do when you got home?

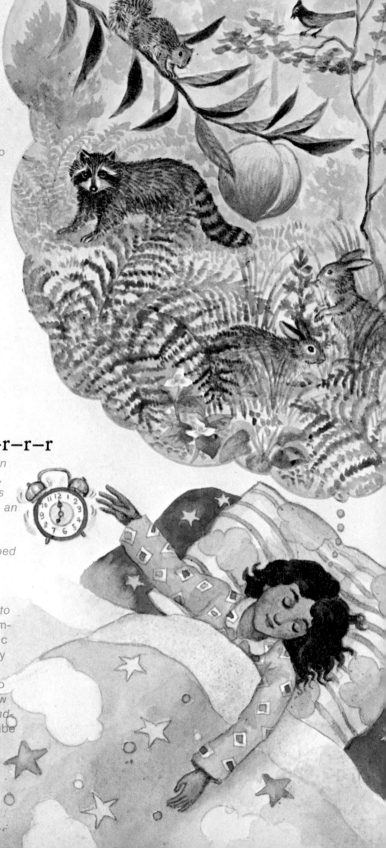

Alarm Clock

A poem by Eve Merriam

Objectives ● To recognize that a poem may have feeling (mood). ● To respond to a poem's mood through another medium.

in the deep sleep forest
there were ferns
there were feathers
there was fur
and a soft ripe peach
on a branch within my

r–r–r–r–r–r–r–r–r–r–r–r–r–r

Introducing the Poem *Sometimes when we are awakened in the middle of a dream, it is hard to tell what is a dream and what is really happening. This poem is about such an experience.*
Discussion Questions *What was this dream about?* (A forest scene.) *What stopped this dream?* (An alarm clock.) *What else might wake you up?* (Possible answers: Mother's voice; a pet; sunshine.)
Enriching Activities **1.** *Fingerpainting to music.* Have the children discuss the dreamlike mood of the poem. Tell them that music often has a dreamlike mood, too. Then play the dream sequence in Tchaikovsky's *Nutcracker Suite,* and have them fingerpaint to the music. Encourage the children to follow the music's tempo as they paint. **2.** *Extending experiences.* Ask the children to describe dreams they have had or have heard.

Picture by Kinuko Craft

212

BOOKSHELF

Strega Nona retold by Tomie de Paola. Prentice Hall, 1975. Strega Nona is a wise old woman with magic powers. Big Anthony helps her with her house and garden until he becomes more interested in finding out how Strega Nona's magic pasta pot works. **Reading Level** Average

Why the Sun and the Moon Live in the Sky by Elphinstone Dayrell. Houghton Mifflin, 1968. Long ago sun, moon, and water all lived on the earth. Sun and moon wanted their friend water to visit, but water with all his people couldn't fit in their house. **Reading Level** Average

The Shoemaker and the Elves retold by the Brothers Grimm. Charles Scribner's Sons, 1960. Each morning a poor shoemaker finds new shoes ready for him to sell. He and his wife wonder who is making the shoes. **Reading Level** Average

The Fire Stealer retold by William Toye. Oxford University Press, 1980. Nanabozho uses magic to bring fire to his people. **Reading Level** Challenging

214

6 We Could Be Friends

We Could Be Friends

A poem by Myra Cohn Livingston

We could be friends
Like friends are supposed to be.
You, picking up the telephone
Calling me

    to come over and play
    or take a walk,
    finding a place
    to sit and talk,

Or just goof around
Like friends do,
Me, picking up the telephone
Calling you.

216

Picture by Susan Lexa

217

Objectives ● To enjoy the humor of a play based on trickery and misunderstandings among the characters. ● To identify character traits by extending a story. ● To perform a play using Story Theater techniques.
Synopsis of the Play A donkey, a dog, a cat, and a rooster travel to Bremen to become musicians. During their journey they discover three robbers feasting inside a house. The hungry animals give a screeching musical concert to frighten the robbers away from their meal. Later that night one of the robbers enters the house, only to be ambushed by the animals. Thinking that goblins are haunting the house, the robbers run away for good.

The Traveling Musicians

A play based on the German folk tale collected by the Brothers Grimm

Pictures by Willi K. Baum

Reading Level Challenging

Characters

Storyteller 1	**Dog**	**Robber 1**
Storyteller 2	**Rooster**	**Robber 2**
Donkey	**Cat**	**Robber 3**

Storyteller 1: Once there was a donkey who had worked for his master for many years. At last he grew too old to carry wheat to the mill. His master did not want him any more.

Donkey:
Pronounced /brem′·ən/. Bremen is a port city in northwestern Germany.

My body is weak, but my voice is still strong. I think I will go to the town of Bremen and sing for my living.

Storyteller 2: So the donkey ran away. On the way to Bremen he met a dog. She was lying by the side of the road panting.

219

Donkey: Why are you out of breath?

Dog: I ran away from my master. He no longer wants me because I am too old to hunt with him. What shall I do now?

Donkey: You may as well come with me, my friend. We will go to Bremen and sing for our living.

Storyteller 1: So the two went on down the road. Before long they met a cat. He was sitting in the middle of the road looking very sad.

Donkey: Why are you so sad, old cat?

Cat: Ah me! My poor old teeth are not as sharp as they used to be. And I'd rather sit by the fire than run after mice. No one wants me, so I'm running away.

Donkey: Come with us to Bremen. The dog and I are going to be musicians. We can all make music together.

Storyteller 2: That made the cat happy, and he went along with the donkey and the dog. After a while they came to a farm. A rooster flew up onto the gate and crowed.

Donkey: What is this noise about? Is something the matter?

Rooster: Cock-a-doodle-doo! This is probably my last crow. For years I woke everyone up in the morning. Now I hear they are planning to make me into soup!

Donkey: What a fine voice you have! Don't stay here and have your head cut off! Come with us! We are going to Bremen to sing for our living. With your voice we shall all make good money.

Storyteller 1: So the four friends went on their way. When night came, they stopped by a big tree to rest.

Storyteller 2: The donkey and the dog lay down under the tree. The cat climbed up into the branches. And the rooster flew to the top of the tree, where he could see all around. Before the others could go to sleep, the rooster called to them.

Rooster: I see lights over there. It must be a house.

Donkey: Let's go there. It will be better than sleeping under this tree.

Dog: And we may find something to eat.

Storyteller 1: So the rooster led them all to the house.

Storyteller 2: When they reached the house, the donkey went to the window. Being the biggest, he could stretch his neck just enough to look inside.

Dog: Well, what do you see?

Donkey: I see three robbers sitting at a table. They are eating dinner. The food looks delicious!

Cat: I would like some of that food. How do you think we might get some?

Rooster: Perhaps together we can think of a plan to frighten away the robbers.

Storyteller 1: So the animals talked together and decided what to do. The donkey kept his place near the window. The dog climbed on the donkey's back. The cat climbed on the dog's back. The rooster flew up to the cat's head. Then they began their music.

All together: Hee—Haaaw! Arf! Arf—arf—arf! Meooow-w-w! Meooow-w-w! Cock-a-doodle-dooo-o!

Storyteller 2: The sound of that music badly frightened the robbers. They ran out the door and into the woods crying,

In folklore, *goblins* (last line of the page) are elflike creatures that are mischievous or evil.

Three Robbers: Run for your life! Goblins are after us!

227

Storyteller 1: When the robbers were gone, the donkey, the dog, the cat, and the rooster went into the house and had a good dinner. Then they all found places to sleep. The cat curled up by the fireplace. The dog lay down beside the door. The donkey stretched out in the yard. The rooster flew to the rooftop. They soon fell fast asleep.

Storyteller 2: About midnight, the robbers came back. The house was dark. Everything was quiet.

Storyteller 1: So one robber went inside to look around. First he went into the kitchen. He saw two bright lights on the floor, and he thought they were coals from the fire.

Robber 1: I'll light a match by this fire. Then I'll be able to see better.

Storyteller 2: But when he bent down, the cat jumped and scratched him on the hand. The robber cried out with fear. He ran to get out the door. There the dog bit the robber in the leg. As he rushed into the yard, the robber was given a big kick by the donkey. Then the rooster woke up and crowed.

Rooster: Cock-a-doodle-doo-o!
Cock-a-doodle-doo-o!

Storyteller 1: The robber ran quickly to tell the others what happened.

Robber 1: Run! Run! The goblins almost killed me! A goblin with long fingernails scratched my hand! Another one cut me in the leg with a knife! Then a big goblin kicked me and knocked me down while a goblin on the roof kept shouting, "Cook him in a stew! Cook him in a stew!"

Pronounced /st(y)ōō/. A *stew* is a thick soup of meat and vegetables cooked together slowly.

Storyteller 2: The robbers lost no time in running far away. This time they didn't come back. As for the donkey, the dog, the cat, and the rooster, they lived together in that house for a long, long time.

Discussion Question · *When the robber returned to the house, each animal did something to frighten him away. How could a goat, a pig, a cow, and a kangaroo have frightened the robber?* (Possible answers: a goat could butt; a pig could grunt; a cow could bite; a kangaroo could box.)

Enriching Activities **1.** *Story Theater.* Have the children perform the play using Story Theater techniques. Some children might read the parts of the storytellers and the characters while others pantomime the characters' actions. See page T42 for Story Theater techniques. **2.** *Music.* Ask the children to mimic the sounds of different animals. Then have them combine their sounds in an animal chorus.

Questions

1. Who were the four musicians?

2. One robber saw two lights. What were the lights?

3. The robber said he heard a goblin shout, "Cook him in a stew." What was *really* said?

4. What do you think is the funniest part of this play?

1. Literal / recall The dog; the cat; the donkey; the rooster. (page 219)
2. Interpretive / inference The cat's eyes. (page 228)
3. Literal / recall "Cock-a-doodle-doo-o!" (page 229)
4. Critical / relating to experience This question is open to personal opinion, so expect different answers from the children.

Activity

The four friends in the story lived together and shared the work. Tell what job each one did. Draw a picture or write one sentence about each animal.

Interpretive / extrapolation *Drawing / writing.* Encourage the children to recall the natural abilities of each animal, but do not discourage imaginative answers.

Learn About

Follow the Road to Bremen

The purpose of the story map is to help the children understand sequence and time and place (setting) in a story.

The four friends in *The Traveling Musicians* traveled the road to Bremen. This story <u>map</u> shows the road and some places along the way.

232

Picture by Willi K. Baum

Objectives ● To match settings with the characters and the action in a story. ● To recognize that a story may have several settings.
Introducing the Lesson *This story map shows the places in* The Traveling Musicians. *Let's trace the musicians' journey.*

Word to Know
   map: a drawing of a country, city, or other region. (page 232)
Discussion Question *In how many places did something happen in the story?* (Six.)
Enriching Activity *Story map.* Have the class use a sheet of butcher paper to make a map for another story, such as *Jack and the Beanstalk* or *The Three Little Pigs.*

Match each sentence below with a place on the story map. Use the letters on the map for answers.

1. The donkey ran away from this place.

2. The donkey met the dog here.

3. The rooster sang his last "Cock-a-doodle-doo" for his master.

4. The four musicians rested here.

5. The donkey and the dog met the cat near this spot.

6. Robbers once lived here.

7. The four musicians never reached this place.

8. The four musicians live here now.

1. Interpretive/ inference A. (pages 218 and 219)
2. Literal/recall B. (pages 218 and 219)

3. Literal/recall D. (page 221)

4. Literal/recall E. (page 223)

5. Literal/recall C. (page 220)

6. Literal/recall F. (page 224)

7. Interpretive/ inference G. (page 230)

8. Literal/recall F. (page 230)

Objectives ● To recognize a problem and a solution in a story. ● To identify solutions to a problem through writing or role playing.
Synopsis of the Story George reluctantly eats all of the split pea soup that his friend Martha makes for him, until one day, in desperation, he pours the soup in his loafers.

Martha sees this, and George confesses that he doesn't like the soup. When Martha tells George that friends should tell each other the truth, George realizes that Martha will still be his friend. Together they decide to eat chocolate chip cookies.

Reading Level Challenging

Split Pea Soup

Story and pictures by James Marshall

Martha was very fond of making split pea soup. Sometimes she made it all day long. Pots and pots of split pea soup.

If there was one thing that George was *not* fond of, it was split pea soup. As a matter of fact, George hated split pea soup more than anything else in the world. But it was so hard to tell Martha.

Introducing the Story   *In this story,*
George does something very silly because he
doesn't want to hurt his friend's feelings. As
we read, think about what you would do if
you were George.

Words to Know
 fond of: like or enjoy. (page 234)
 split pea soup: a soup made with peas.
   (page 234)

235

One day after George had eaten ten bowls of Martha's soup, he said to himself, "I just can't stand another bowl. Not even another spoonful."

So, while Martha was out in the kitchen, George carefully poured the rest of his soup into his loafers under the table. "Now she will think I have eaten it."

Loafers are a kind of shoe.

But Martha was watching from the kitchen.

Before the children
read this page, they
might discuss what
they think Martha
should do about the
situation.

"How do you expect to walk home with your loafers full of split pea soup?" she asked George.

"Oh, dear," said George. "You saw me."

"And why didn't you tell me that you hate my split pea soup?"

"I didn't want to hurt your feelings," said George.

"That's silly," said Martha. "Friends should always tell each other the truth. As a matter of fact, I don't like split pea soup very much myself. I only like to make it. From now on, you'll never have to eat that awful soup again."

Ask for the meaning of
"What a relief!"

"What a relief!" George sighed.

"Would you like some chocolate chip cookies instead?" asked Martha.

"Oh, that would be lovely," said George.

"Then you shall have them," said his friend.

Questions

1. Why didn't George eat the split pea soup?

2. What did Martha tell George that he should have done?

3. What did George wear on his feet?
   soup   boots   loafers

4. The next time George eats at Martha's house, what could she cook for him?

Activity

Finish the play. Your friend wants you to do something you don't want to do. What does your friend say? What will you answer? Write as much as you wish.

Friend: I want you to ＿＿＿＿＿＿.

Me: ＿＿＿＿＿＿＿＿＿.

From

Grandfather

A poem by Shirley Crawford

Grandfather sings, I dance.

Grandfather speaks, I listen.

Now I sing, who will dance?

I speak, who will listen?

Grandfather hunts, I learn.

Grandfather fishes, I clean.

Now I hunt, who will learn?

I fish, who will clean?

See page T58 for the final stanza of "Grandfather."

Picture by Konrad Hack

Objectives • To infer reasons for a change in a character's attitude. • To recognize that friendship grows through shared experiences.

Synopsis of the Story Though not welcomed at first by the class, a new girl named Crystal soon proves to be friendly, funny, and mischievous. Her pranks bring mild trouble with the teacher or the principal, but each strengthens the friendship between Crystal and Susan. At the end of the school year, Crystal leaves for the summer and Susan eagerly anticipates the fall, when she can be with Crystal again.

Introducing the Story *Try to remember when you met your best friend for the first time. Did you like each other right away? In this story, Susan tells about a new girl in her school, whom she doesn't like. Read what happens as Susan gets to know Crystal.*

Words to Know
amnesia (am·nē′·zhə): a loss of memory. (page 244)
telescope: an instrument that makes far-off things look nearer and larger. (page 249)
scrapbook: a book of blank pages for pictures, clippings, and souvenirs. (page 252)

Crystal Is the New Girl

Adapted from the story by Shirley Gordon   **Reading Level** Average

Pictures by Dora Leder

Crystal is the new girl in our school. We all stare at her when she comes into class. Nobody in school is friends with Crystal. Crystal acts like she doesn't care.

The teacher tells Crystal to sit next to me. "I hope you and Crystal will learn to be friends, Susan," the teacher tells me. I don't want to learn to be Crystal's friend.

243

"What's your name? What's your name?"
Crystal keeps asking me.

"You know my name is Susan," I keep
telling her.

"I just want to make sure you don't
catch *amnesia*," Crystal says.

Crystal smiles, but I don't smile back.

The teacher tells Crystal and me to *Hush!*

"The teacher was cross," I tell my mother after school, "because Crystal was talking to me in class."

"Who is Crystal?" my mother asks.

"Crystal is the new girl in school," I explain.

"Oh, it's nice you have a new friend."

"Crystal isn't my friend," I tell my mother.

Crystal is wearing her sunglasses in
class. She doesn't want to take them off.
"I can see New York with them," says
Crystal.

"No, you can't," I tell her.

Crystal smiles at me and says, "San
Francisco?"

I try not to smile, but I can't help it.

"Shhhh!" The teacher looks down
his nose at Crystal and me.

"The teacher was cross again," I tell my mother after school, "because Crystal was talking to me in class."

"Crystal shouldn't talk in class," my mother tells me.

"Crystal says funny things," I tell my mother.

Crystal and I are taking a test. Crystal whispers at me, "Don't let me see your paper. That would be cheating."

I make a face at Crystal, and she makes a face back at me.

The teacher shakes his head at us and says, "Ah-ah-ah!"

"Crystal and I were sent to the principal's office today," I tell my mother after school.

"You and Crystal shouldn't get into so much trouble."

"Crystal and I are friends," I tell my mother.

Crystal rolls up her paper like a telescope. She holds it up to her eye and squints through it at the sun outside the window. "It's time for lunch," Crystal says.

The teacher looks at us. Then he looks at his watch and says, "It's time for lunch."

Crystal and I sit on the playground and open our lunch boxes. Crystal's lunch is bologna and mine is peanut butter and jelly.

Bologna /bə·lō'·nē/ is a luncheon meat.

"I'll trade you half of mine for half of yours," says Crystal.

249

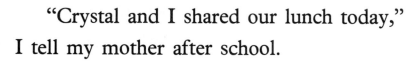

"Crystal and I shared our lunch today,"
I tell my mother after school.

"That's nice."

"Crystal and I are going to be friends
forever," I tell my mother.

"Sss-sss!" Crystal hisses at me like a
snake.

"Shhh," I tell her. "We can't talk in
class."

"Snakes don't talk," says Crystal.
Crystal giggles, and I giggle with her.

The teacher clucks his tongue at us
and makes a noise like *Tsk-tsk-tsk!*

"The teacher won't let Crystal and me
sit together anymore," I tell my mother
after school.

"That's too bad."

"Crystal and I are still friends," I
tell my mother.

It is summer, and the last day of
school. I look across the room at Crystal.
She is wearing two new hair ribbons. One
is red and one is green. Crystal smiles
at me and calls out, "Merry Christmas!"

The teacher looks at us and says,
"Class dismissed."

My mother takes a picture of Crystal and me for my scrapbook. Then Crystal's mother comes to drive her home.

"I wish Crystal lived next door to us," I tell my mother.

"You'll see Crystal again when school starts in the fall."

Crystal's face in the car window gets smaller and smaller.

"Don't catch amnesia and forget me!" hollers Crystal.

I wish there was school tomorrow.

Questions

1. What was one thing Crystal and Susan did to become friends?

2. If Crystal looks at Susan's paper during a test, what might someone think she is doing?

    talking   giggling   cheating

3. Why did Susan say, "I wish there was school tomorrow"?

4. What do you think happened to Susan and Crystal the next year?

Activity

A new person has come to your class. Write three things you might do to make that person feel welcome.

253

Spinning Song

A poem by Zilpha Keatley Snyder

254

The bar is smooth
        beneath our knees,
Our hands are strong,
        we sit at ease,
And when we're set
        we grab hold tight,
And back we spin
        with all our might.
The bar gets hot—
        around, around—
Our flying hair
        whips air and ground.
Of all who spin
        on playground bars,
We are the best!
        we are the stars!
Jeanette's my friend,
        and it is she,
Who always goes
        around with me.

Picture by Susan Lexa

BOOKSHELF

Best Friends for Frances by Russell Hoban. Harper & Row, 1969. Frances is angry with her best friend Albert. She makes her sister Gloria her best friend and starts to go with her on a picnic. Albert is upset. He wants to go, too. **Reading Level** Average

The Shy Little Girl by Phyllis Krasilovsky. Houghton Mifflin, 1970. Anne is shy and quiet. She never raises her hand in school. She never jumps rope with other children. She is always by herself until the new girl comes to school. **Reading Level** Challenging

Amigo by Byrd Baylor Schweitzer. Macmillan, 1963. Francisco wants a dog, a dog he can call Amigo. Then he meets a prairie dog puppy who wants a boy. **Reading Level** Challenging

Nate the Great and the Sticky Case by Marjorie Weinman Sharmat. Coward, McCann & Geoghegan, 1978. Nate tries to help his friend Claude find his lost stegosaurus stamp. **Reading Level** Easy